Author's Preface

This is a true story of a poor Victorian family; it is my grandmother's life-story. The family tales she told me I have reiterated to the best of my ability, verifying them with other family members. Dates of births and deaths, and historical events, such as the mine disaster, I have researched at Bristol Registry, National Archives and local newspapers.

All the characters in the book are true, and hopefully bear resemblance to the people they represent. None of the names of my relatives have been changed; other incidental characters have been given fictional names, unless I have been able to obtain consent to use real names from their descendents.

I have not attempted to reproduce the Bristolian dialect; even today's Bristolians would not comprehend it. As late as the nineteen-fifties I can recall my Grandmother using 'thee' and 'thou' in her everyday speech. For some unknown reason, it is one of the dialects which was suppressed shortly after the last war; perhaps Bristolians saw themselves as too sophisticated to use it.

My thanks are due to Pat Hase, who kindled my enthusiasm, the Hanham History Society for their help, Bristol and Avon Family History Society and Weston-super-Mare Family History Society for use of their facilities. Thanks also to my mother, Edna, Aunt Ivy, Amy (now deceased), my sister, Pat, and my cousin Joyce for photos and reminiscences, my husband and children for their constant encouragement, especially my daughter, Kim, who has acted as my reader and designer and without whom this book would never have been completed.

HARRIET'S FAMILY

Sheila Hayward

Order this book online at www.trafford.com/08-0592
or email orders@trafford.com

Most Trafford titles are also available at major online book retailers.

© Copyright 2008 Sheila Hayward.

All rights reserved. No part of this publication may be reproduced, stored in a retrieval system, or transmitted, in any form or by any means, electronic, mechanical, photocopying, recording, or otherwise, without the written prior permission of the author.

Edited by: Kim Davies
Cover Design by: Kim Davies

Note for Librarians: A cataloguing record for this book is available from Library and Archives Canada at www.collectionscanada.ca/amicus/index-e.html

Printed in Victoria, BC, Canada.

ISBN: 978-1-4251-7784-3

We at Trafford believe that it is the responsibility of us all, as both individuals and corporations, to make choices that are environmentally and socially sound. You, in turn, are supporting this responsible conduct each time you purchase a Trafford book, or make use of our publishing services. To find out how you are helping, please visit www.trafford.com/responsiblepublishing.html

Our mission is to efficiently provide the world's finest, most comprehensive book publishing service, enabling every author to experience success. To find out how to publish your book, your way, and have it available worldwide, visit us online at www.trafford.com/10510

www.trafford.com

North America & international
toll-free: 1 888 232 4444 (USA & Canada)
phone: 250 383 6864 ♦ fax: 250 383 6804
email: info@trafford.com

The United Kingdom & Europe
phone: +44 (0)1865 722 113 ♦ local rate: 0845 230 9601
facsimile: +44 (0)1865 722 868 ♦ email: info.uk@trafford.com

10 9 8 7 6 5 4 3

For my children, Kim, Tania, Robert and Emma, their children and their children's children, ad infinitum

Chapter 1

CHILDHOOD

THE THIN, piercing wail of a newborn child threaded its way down the narrow stairs of the dim, terraced house, greeting George Bolt as he pushed open the front door of 10 Francis Place. The Bedminster area of Bristol, in 1882, could best be described as 'grey'. The houses were grey, the pavements and roads were grey, the people wore grey, downtrodden faces and drab clothing in shades of brown, black and, inevitably, grey. It was a hive of industrial activity, in spite of its greyness, but the activity was not an indicator of enjoyment which the workers derived from their employ, which was often long, arduous and poorly paid.

George, a stocky-built young man of twenty-two, was a labourer at Williams & Boucher, the nearby sawmills. He quickened his step. He had known Sarah was in labour when he had left for work in the morning and had called his mother who had promised to look after his wife during the birth. It was their first child.

His mother was descending the stairs into the kitchen. 'It's a boy,' she said, obviously pleased. She herself had only raised one boy together with five daughters, her other son had died before his first birthday. All men wanted sons, she reasoned. 'You can go on upstairs, the midwife is with her, so knock before you go in. Your dinner's on the stove.'

The midwife emerged from the bedroom as he reached the door, carrying a bundle of washing. She lived nearby, and attended all the births in the locality.

'No bills this time, George, we haven't had to call a doctor. It wasn't that easy, but they are both well.'

Sarah was lying in bed, looking tired, holding a small bundle in the crook of her arm. Her long, dark hair hung damply about her face; her eyes smiled although her facial muscles were too exhausted. George peered at the baby and kissed Sarah on the head.

'Little George. I knew it would be a boy. Are you all right, Sarah?' His eyes glowed and he exuded a warmth that enveloped all three of them. It was taken for granted that George would be the boy's name, after his father and grandfather before him. 'The start of our family, Sarah. By God, I shall be proud of my family. And you shall be proud of me. I'll work hard, I won't always be a labourer all my life. Old Alf said today he will teach me the wheelwright trade. We sha'n't always live in rented rooms. You and the children will ride out in a carriage on Sundays, just as you've always wanted, you'll see.'

'How about calling him George Henry, give him two names?' suggested Sarah. She had two Christian names, she was Sarah Jane.

'Why Henry?' asked George, surprised but not displeased. Sarah's father's name was Fredrick, although he knew Sarah did not think too highly of her father.

'I just like the name; I think it would be nice to have something of his own,' she replied. In fact, one of her brothers was called Henry, he was the only member of the Herbert family to make a success of reading and writing, and had a white-collar job as a clerk. Sarah was secretly proud of her brother Henry, but it would not do to say so to her husband, however George was not a stupid man, he made the connection for himself, but did not comment.

The midwife reappeared in the room, took the baby and laid him in the swinging cradle, loaned by one of George's relatives.

'I shall be off now. Don't let your wife get out of bed at all, or do anything other than feed the baby, and don't do that before nine o'clock tonight or he'll get colic,' she admonished. She went down the stairs and into the street, where the grey November night was closing in. There were no gas street-lights in the side roads, and she picked her way by the dim light emanating from the dwellings.

At that time the city docks ran as far as Bedminster; in the previous century Bristol had been the third point of a thriving sugar-slave trade. Trade with the West Indies and other foreign ports was still maintained, and there was a brisk trade with the South Wales ports, whose boats loaded and unloaded at Welsh Back. George's father-in-law, Fredrick Herbert, was a mariner, who frequently signed for the Welsh trade, preferring shorter trips now that he was older. In addition to signing on for work on the ships, there was always casual labour to be found unloading and loading cargo. This held no security, being paid at day-rates, and was largely unregulated, so employers acknowledged no responsibility for deaths or accidents.

Numerous sawmills and manufacturing industries, whose raw materials came through the Bristol Docks, were centred in Bristol, many in Bedminster and the adjoining areas. The legacy of the sugar trade had founded several sugar refineries in Bristol, one of the most prominent being that of Conrad Finzel, a German by origin. He was deeply committed to his adopted city, not only providing employment and care for his employees, but sending a proportion of his factory's profits to the Bristol orphanage founded by his compatriot, Muller. However, the bigger ships now used to transport the sugar from the West Indies could not negotiate Bristol docks entrance, and the trade was moving to Liverpool and other larger docks. George's father had worked as a labourer at Finzel's, until shortly before his disappearance.

'You go downstairs and have your tea now, George' Sarah urged. 'Your mother has cooked you something.' As she settled back on her pillow she thought of her own mother, who had died at the age of forty-eight when Sarah was nine years old. Being the youngest of six children she had never witnessed her own mother with a baby. But she remembered her mother as constantly tired, careworn and anxious about money. Her father was often away at sea; when home he was irascible and Sarah lived in fear of him. She sighed, hoping that her life would have more rewards than her mother's.

George descended the stairs and sat at the kitchen table, where his mother placed a plate of stew before him. Although money was not plentiful, somehow his mother and Sarah always contrived a meal at the end of the day.

As he ate, George thought about his father. He remembered coming home from school—he must have been eight years old then—to find his mother sitting at the kitchen table, red-rimmed eyes and set face. 'Your father's gone,' she said, 'I don't think we'll see him no more.' She would give no further information to George or his sisters as to why their father had left.

They were living in Clark Street at the time, in a house his parents had always rented; all the children had been born there. His mother had been pregnant with Elizabeth when their father left home, although George had not known that at the time, as pregnancy was a matter not discussed with the children. George recalled how he had searched Bedminster for his father, day after day. He loitered at the factory gates when the whistle blew in the evening, scanning the faces; he saw one or two of his father's old friends, but they avoided his gaze. On one occasion he grabbed the coat of one: 'Mr, Bates, Mr Bates, have you seen my dad?'

The man had shaken him off, roughly. 'No I ain't, go on home, young George, or I'll tell your mother you're down here every night.'

George had run home then, not because he was afraid of his mother's sharp tongue, but because he did not want to cause her any further anxiety. He knew that his mother was finding it hard to keep the family home together. His father's brothers had called at the house several times, and there were whispered conversations in the front parlour, but none of them were wealthy men; with families of their own they had little cash to spare. Within six months of their father leaving home the two older girls, Sally and

Maria, found jobs. Fourteen-year-old Sally went into service with a plumber's family in North Street; Mr Worrinder had benefited financially from Bristol Corporation's drive to ensure all dwellings in Bristol and Bedminster had piped water supplies.

'I've got a room of my own, and it's always warm in the house and I've plenty to eat,' she told George one day, when she met him in North Street. She was pushing the pram with Baby Worrinder in it. 'They've only got this one baby for me to look after, so it's not such hard work as it was at home.'

Maria, age thirteen, found a job at the local bookbinders. His mother had tried hard to keep the family home together. George offered to leave school early, but his mother would not hear of it. 'You'll stay at school till you're twelve, same as the others, even if I have to go out scrubbing floors,' she said, and she did. He had left school at twelve and found a job as a labourer. Julia became pregnant and was married at sixteen, much to her family's dismay. Alice found work at a local factory, making throat lozenges, when she was fourteen, to be followed two years later by Elizabeth.

It was during the course of one of her cleaning jobs that George's mother met Thomas Jupe. He was a retired soldier, who was discharged from the army when he lost a leg fighting in Africa. He decided against living in London as a Chelsea Pensioner, and returned to the West Country where he had been born. He managed well with a wooden leg, and paid Mrs Bolt to clean his house and cook him one meal a day.

He had assumed that Mrs Bolt was a widow, and one day said to her, 'Mrs Bolt, we get on well together, would you do me the honour of becoming my wife?'

She was speechless for a moment. She had always regarded Thomas as a confirmed old bachelor. She fudged an answer, saying she would have to think about it because of the children. A few days later Thomas repeated his offer. 'I would be happy for the children to come and live here too,' he added, 'it's not as though they are little children who would disturb me.' Elizabeth, the youngest, was nine years old by that time.

'It's not quite that simple, Mr Jupe,' said Mrs Bolt. 'My husband is still alive somewhere, so I can't marry again. I have no idea where he is. He left me when I was expecting Elizabeth. Said he couldn't stand any more children, wanted to be a free man again and off he went.'

'So you have held your family together all that time, without help?' asked Thomas, full of admiration.

'No, the first year or so my husband's brothers and my brothers helped me with a little money, but none of them are well-off and they have families of their own. As soon as I could leave the children to look after each other I found work and supported us myself.'

'Well, said Thomas, 'my offer still holds good. How about simply moving in with me, we can tell my neighbours we got married. I am sure you and your family will be happy here.'

Mrs Bolt agreed. She took his surname, and Thomas's neighbours believed they were married. George and his two younger sisters, Elizabeth and Alice, moved in too; Maria had recently married and moved to London. George did not resent his mother's situation, as it meant she no longer had to earn money doing other families' housework. The children grew to respect Mr Jupe, who was an honest man and genuinely fond of their mother. Young George, at fourteen, had been fascinated by Thomas's stories of Africa and wars—and Thomas was delighted to have an audience.

As George finished eating, Thomas Jupe came in from the street. 'Is it all done then?' he asked.

'Yes it's a boy, Mr Jupe,' George replied. Thomas grunted and flopped into the chair near the stove, while George's mother began to put up his meal. He had spent the day at the old-soldiers almshouse, where he had some friends, so as not to be in the house during the birth. Childbirth was for women; Thomas had never had children of his own.

For a few months all went well in the household, but as winter set in and Thomas Jupe was frequently fighting his way to the stove through a barrier of drying napkins, he became increasingly taciturn.

'He's never had a family or young children about him,' Mrs Bolt tried to reassure Sarah. 'Don't worry about it, he will get used to it.'

But Sarah did worry. She also felt that the house had become very overcrowded with the addition of one small mortal. There was only one large room downstairs, where they all cooked, ate and sat, apart from the scullery at the back where the washing was boiled. Upstairs was one bedroom, where Mr Jupe and Mrs Bolt slept; the stairs came into the other room, which was partitioned by a curtain. She and George slept one side of the curtain and his two sisters the other side.

'No one in the house has room to move, let alone any privacy,' Sarah told her eldest sister Harriet, over a cup of tea one afternoon. She had arrived at Harriet's house unannounced because baby George Henry was in a fitful stage and would not stop crying. Thomas Jupe had asked several times if they were to get any peace, so Mrs Bolt had told Sarah to leave the washing which she would finish, and take the baby for a walk. It had begun to rain as Sarah walked to her sister's carrying her child.

'I can't keep doing this every time he cries, not through the winter,' she said. 'Besides, he's getting heavier all the time. I could do with a pram; do you know anyone who would lend me one? Not that we've anywhere to put it, so I s'pose that would be wrong too.'

'Have you talked to George about this?' asked Harriet, still busily plying her needle as she talked and drank tea. Harriet had been employed as a needlewoman at the age of twelve; twenty-two years later she was self-employed, taking outwork from a number of Bristol tailors and was also a skilled cutter.

'I tried,' replied Sarah, 'but he just said surely you and my mother can manage one small baby and one old man between you. You see, we pay practically nothing in rent, and George says that's all he can afford.'

Harriet laughed so heartily that Sarah laughed too.

'Men,' said Harriet, 'they've no idea what goes on in the home, do they. Now, why don't you and George come and live here? My Tom will be away for a few more years yet; by then you will be able to afford a place of your own. You can always help me with sewing instead of paying rent, I can teach you the trade, and you can put a bit of money aside.'

Harriet's husband Tom Martin had spent almost all of his married life in prison. Harriet married him shortly after her mother had died, partly because Tom was an attractive young tearaway with a circle of admiring friends and partly because Harriet could not bear to live under her father's roof once her mother had died. Tom had already been in prison for six months for theft the year before their wedding, but Harriet was sure that a good wife would keep him on the straight-and-narrow. She was wrong. Within a year Tom appeared in court again for stealing and on that occasion was sentenced to seven years imprisonment. He returned home in 1876 but had difficulty finding a job so once again turned to stealing; was caught and returned to jail for a further ten years. As Harriet said, he's never home long enough to father children. Fortunately she had a trade and was able to support herself; she was an astute businesswoman and respected by the local tailors.

Sarah felt as though a weight had been lifted from her heart, she leaned forward and kissed her sister on the cheek, disturbing the baby who protested, then dropped off to sleep again. 'Do you really mean it, Harriet? It sounds like heaven to me.' Tears sprang into Sarah's eyes.

'Now you go home and talk to George about it,' said Harriet, 'come back tomorrow and tell me what he said.'

Sarah could hardly wait for George to come home from work. She was afraid they would have no privacy to discuss Harriet's suggestion, but fortunately Mr Jupe ate his tea and went out for the evening. Sarah was happy to include Mrs Bolt in the discussion.

George was a little surprised; he didn't see what all the fuss was about. 'Is it worth the bother of moving, Sarah?' he asked. 'It will still be rented rooms, not like having a house of our own.'

'Yes but it won't be so overcrowded as it is here,' said Sarah. 'We can have the landing room all to ourselves, there will be plenty of room for our bed and the baby's cot.'

'I think it's a good idea, George,' his mother said. 'Your son is getting bigger every day. Imagine when he's crawling around the floor, which won't be many months now—Thomas would be falling over him! He's getting less steady on that wooden leg than he used to be!'

Sarah produced the final argument: 'Apart from that, I think I'm going to have another baby.'

George caved in and the following Sunday borrowed a horse and cart from work to move their few belongings to Percy Street, a short distance away.

Sarah was so happy to be living with her sister; she immediately began to learn all that Harriet could teach her about sewing and tailoring. When she had completed more than the agreed amount of sewing to pay their rent, Harriet paid her for extra work, which Sarah saved in a biscuit tin.

Seven months later, William John was born, named after George's Uncle William and his grandfather, John Bolt. Harriet looked after Sarah during her lying-in period and Sarah felt her debt of gratitude deepen.

'If I ever have a child you can do the same for me,' Harriet dismissed thanks with a wave of her hand.

William was a fine boy and George was very proud of his two sons. Sarah found that she had her hands full with two young children and was hard pushed to complete her quota of sewing to pay their rent, so George had to supplement this with cash. Sarah was feeling run-down, with so much work; both of the children had colds which developed into coughs. Sarah blamed herself, with hindsight, that had she not been feeling ill herself she would have noticed that little William's cough was getting worse, not better after several weeks. After a sleepless night of coughing, it was George, bleary-eyed, who threw some coins on the kitchen table and said to Sarah, 'For goodness sake, take that baby to the doctor's and get something for him.'

Sarah had tried a patent medicine, but now did as George bid her. Dr Norton's face was grave as he listened to little William's chest through the stethoscope.

'How long has he had the cough?'

'About a month, doctor,' Sarah replied, realising that it was nearer six weeks.

'Well his lungs sound very congested, I think he has a severe chest infection. Give him this medicine three times a day. Keep him warm, but don't overheat the room. A smoky, stuffy room will not be good for him, so don't put him in the room by the kitchen stove. If he's no better in a week, bring him back to see me.'

Worried, Sarah took the baby home. He could not stay upstairs in their bedroom so as to avoid the smoke from the kitchen stove, as it was a cold damp November and there was no fireplace in their bedroom; the kitchen was the only warm room in the house. The medicine seemed to make no difference, William still coughed, cried and gasped for breath. Sleepless nights became part of their lives. In the middle of a particularly bad night Sarah determined to take William back to the doctor the next day. She dropped off to sleep just before dawn and dragged herself out of bed when she heard George stirring to go to work. The baby was quiet, must have tired himself out, she thought, and glanced in the cot. He was still and white; Sarah realised at once that he was dead. He was eight months old.

Dr Norton wrote 'bronchitis' on the baby's death certificate, a term Sarah had heard before in conjunction with children's deaths, but never had she experienced it so close to home. She was inconsolable and blamed herself—for what, she knew not. George, too, was upset; he had been proud to have fathered another son, but soon his hurt healed and he was weary of Sarah's grief, telling her to pull herself together. It was George Henry who was Sarah's consolation, and gradually life returned to normal.

Six months later Sarah found she was pregnant again. Although she realised that no-one would ever replace William, she rejoiced in the idea of having another baby. George Henry would be three years old by the time the baby was born, a nice gap between siblings.

The little girl was born on February 24th 1885 and Sarah named her Harriet Jane, after her sister who had been such a prop and role model in her life, and their beloved mother, who was also Harriet. She was a little scrap of a thing, compared to the birth size of the two sons, but she possessed a hearty pair of lungs and a determination to be noticed in the world.

George, true to his promise, was working hard at the timber yard, and had moved up a step, from labourer to sawyer; he had his sights set on the foreman's job, when old Bill retired. He was occasionally asked to help with costings and was extremely grateful that his mother had ensured he had some education, at no small sacrifice to the family at that time, for education was not cheap or easy to come by when he was a lad. Free now, it was, and compulsory. But could it be any good if it was free? George resolved to send his children to the Church School, and pay the penny a week asked; even the girl should go there, although she would only get married. Still, he reasoned, no man worth his salt would want his wife totally uneducated. But George Henry should have a proper education then he would not have to take a labourer's job. Perhaps a white-collar job, like his Uncle Henry? George was not a stupid man, he had made the connection for himself.

George Henry was greatly entertained by his young sister, who as she grew old enough to crawl, then walk, followed him unceasingly. Sarah found her daughter an easier baby to manage than William had been and was able to resume her sewing and tailoring.

When Baby Harriet was just over a year old, Harriet received a letter. This was an unusual event in that few letters arrived in Percy Street. Neither Sarah nor Harriet could read or write and had to wait until George came home from work, to find out the contents.

He read the letter aloud, haltingly, for it contained a number of unfamiliar words.

'Well, good news for you, Harriet, bad news for us, as we shall have to move out,' he said. Tom Martin was to be released from prison the following month, a year early for good behaviour. 'Sarah, you'd better start looking for a house for us to rent, you know what we can afford.'

'It will only be good news if he stays on good behaviour once he's out,' replied Harriet, stunned at the news.

Sarah began next day, searching for a house to rent. She did not want to rent rooms in a shared house, if she could possibly avoid it, and wanted to find a house with piped water and if possible their own toilet, rather than shared. Everything she found which she liked was too expensive; those they could afford were cramped, damp, or both.

Sarah's brother Jack called to see her and George one evening. Jack was unmarried and suffered from asthma and a chronic cough, but managed to hold down a job at the local shoe factory. He had lived with their elder brother, Peter, since Peter's marriage.

'I was wondering, Sarah, if you get a house of your own, whether I could come and live with you,' he said. 'Peter's wife is due for another baby next month, that will be their seventh, and there isn't really room for me any longer. I'll pay good money for my bed and board, which will help with your rent.'

Sarah looked at George hopefully; this could be the extra cash they needed to find them a home of their own. George rubbed his chin as he thought.

'Well we hadn't really reckoned on anyone else living with us Jack, but if it would help you out, then that should be fine with us.' He glanced at Sarah, who smiled, but thought how typical, he would not admit to needing the money. Sarah wasted no time and within a month had found a cottage to rent in New Margaret

Place, just across Bristol Bridge from George's workplace. The cottage boasted a small front parlour, which was to be Jack's bedroom; as Sarah had no parlour furniture it was no loss to the family. By the time they moved in Sarah was pregnant again.

Harriet was a quiet child, watching the world with her blue eyes, set in a round, pale face, surrounded by dark hair—'pump-water straight', Sarah called her daughter's hair; there was not a ripple of a wave in it, but it was fine and soft. Harriet attached herself to her mother's skirt and learned the tasks of a woman early in her life, while her brother George Henry took advantage of his masculine freedom to roam the Bedminster environment and make friends at his new school.

'When you are big like me you will be able to go to school too,' he told Harriet. She loved his stories about school, and listened wide-eyed to accounts of bad boys who were given the cane.

'I can read, too,' said George Henry, and impressed the whole family by reading most of a passage from one of the religious tracts supplied by Uncle Cornelius. He was proving himself an able pupil and George was proud of his son.

Harriet listened to her mother talking to friends and relatives, and played happily with any children they brought with them. When the baby, Alice Rosina, was born, two-year old Harriet was delighted, and took a proprietary interest, fetching nappies and clean clothes for her, and rocking the 'borrowed' cradle, which by now was a permanent feature in the Bolt household, having sheltered four babies in five years.

With three young children, Sarah was always busy, and only able to take a limited amount of work from the tailor. Money was very tight, and Sarah had to use all her ingenuity and management skills to keep the family home as she wanted. Harriet watched and learned; by five years of age she was a passable cook and washerwoman, under her mother's supervision. A mid-day meal had to be cooked for the family, and one of Harriet's duties was to put her father's meal in a basin and run to the sawmills with it before it became cold. George insisted on a cooked meal at mid-day, but did not have time to return home for it. When the children were at school, either George or Harriet had to run to the sawmills and back before having their own meal, which often made them late for afternoon school. As George was older, and his education was deemed more important than Harriet's, the 'dinner run' was her job. Frequently, then, she did not return for afternoon school, but stayed home to help with household chores, so that her mother could sew.

More and more, Harriet was kept home from school to help with chores. She saw her classmates, and even her younger sister, learning things of which she had no knowledge. Mondays, as washing-days, were out of the question as schooldays.

'Please let me go today, they are learning long-division,' Harriet would plead with her mother.

'I can't spare you today, there's sheets to wash, and I have to finish these overcoats by four o'clock,' Sarah replied. 'Besides, why would you want to learn that? You can read and write, more than I could do by your age, and you can reckon money better than most adults I know. There's plenty of years left to go to school.' Sarah would not admit that she could not read or write, even to her family.

Sarah frequently sent messages to school that Harriet was ill, and she gained an unwarranted reputation as a sickly child, whereas in reality she cooked and did housework while Sarah sat at the treadle sewing-machine, a second-hand purchase from her sister. Dust from the dressing in the fabric made her cough, but she worked on while her husband was at work, because another, more sinister reason was curtailing the family's available funds.

George was good at his job; he was reliable and intelligent enough to assimilate and retain information relevant to his job and interests. He was also good at drawing and was sometimes asked to make designs for carts and carriages which Williams and Boucher made. He had been promoted to foreman, and was sent on buying trips to select trees for purchase, for specific orders. Pressures began to build; although George knew his job, and enjoyed a challenge, his schooling had been rudimentary. Paperwork and figures began to feature more prominently in his life. In addition, pressures came from his former workmates, whom he was now supervising.

'Too grand to come and have a drink with us, then, George?' they ribbed. George began to drink more regularly and more heavily. Frequently he went to the pub after the final hooter had blown, and did not return home until closing time. He was not alone in this; many of his fellow workers and neighbours followed the same ritual. This time-lapse also ensured that their wives had the children in bed by the time they returned. While George would still protest that he loved his children, he no longer enjoyed the noisy domesticity which accompanied their early training.

When George drank, he became aggressive. He was a strong, broad-shouldered man, and none of the other men would have challenged him, so he took his aggression home. The fear of pregnancy made Sarah avoid sex with her husband. This avoidance angered George, who, although he was not actively seeking more children, saw marital sex as his right. It was his wife's duty, and her responsibility to avoid becoming pregnant by whatever means there were, he reasoned. At the time, reliable means amounted to very little. Many women of Sarah's acquaintance resorted to trying self-induced abortions; one of Sarah's neighbours had bled to death as a result.

With a few drinks inside him, George's anger at Sarah's reticence brought out his aggression towards her. He found that if he attacked her physically, she became compliant, or tried to appease him with affection. It was a game neither consciously realised they played.

Many mornings, in the cold light of dawn, he looked at Sarah's bruises with remorse and muttered 'Did I really do that, Sarah? It was the drink, not me.' But it didn't stop him drinking the next evening.

Sarah's brother Jack had tried to intervene one evening when he happened to be in the kitchen.

'Don't you tell me what to do in my own house, with my own wife,' shouted George. 'If you don't like it here, you move out.'

Sarah hushed her brother; she was unwilling to lose Jack's housekeeping money and knew that if Jack left, George's violence would still continue. She spoke to her brother next day.

'Don't you worry about me Jack. He's all shouting and noise, he very rarely comes to blows. If you hear him, stay in your own room, just ignore him. I can manage him.' This was a lie, but it was what she wanted her brother to think. So Jack stayed in his room at night. His health was deteriorating; he came home from work and managed to eat the meal Sarah had prepared him, then he sat by the stove, coughing almost continuously until it eight o'clock, when it was time for his night-time medication. This was sedative and he retired to bed shortly afterwards, long before George returned from the public house. Generally his drug-induced sleep prevented him hearing domestic upheavals.

Harriet, as a small child, had seen many neighbourhood women with bruises and black eyes, and had gleaned the cause, from whisperings and gossip among the women. Then, in bed at night, she began to hear raised voices when her father came home, and loud noises. The next day her mother would be sporting bruises, as the other women in the street. On one occasion, when Harriet was six years old, she heard raised voices, and crept to the bend of the stairs; the door at the bottom of the stairs was open. She saw her father, with his fist raised; her mother, although heavily pregnant, dodged behind the kitchen table. George pursued her; Sarah ran—slipped and fell heavily. She screamed. Harriet's brother, George Henry, joined Harriet at the top of the stairs.

'Sshhh,' said Harriet. 'Our father was chasing our mother and she's fell over. I don't think he can get her up off the floor.' George, drunk and largely incapable of keeping himself upright, was cursing at the recumbent Sarah, as he tried to haul her to her feet.

'Oh God, be careful, George,' she kept repeating.

Alice, who was only four years old at the time, was woken by the noise and began to cry. George suddenly caught sight of the two children on the stairs. 'Get back to bed!' he bellowed. 'Shut that child up! I don't want to hear another sound from any of you. My God, can't a man have a bit of peace in his own house on a night?'

The children retreated to bed. George, sobered by the events of the past ten minutes, helped Sarah to bed. However, during the night, Sarah started labour, six weeks before her time. George had to call the doctor to the house, and the precipitating events had to be divulged to him.

'George Bolt,' he said, 'if I didn't know you better, I'd have you put in prison for this. Look what you've done; likely as not, she will lose the baby.'

In the cold light of dawn, George was contrite. He did what he could to make Sarah comfortable before going to work, even called at his mother's to ask her to come and look after Sarah during the day. In a sober frame of mind, George loved his wife, and treated her as well as most working-class wives expected, but when he had taken a few drinks, all kindness and reason seemed to leave him. Sarah was confined to bed for the day, but next day baby Florence was born, and only lived a few days.

Two years later, Richard was born, and again only survived a few days. Sarah, distraught, began to wonder if she would ever bear another child who lived. Was her life solely to be a round of pregnancy, birth and death?

Harriet had been too young to comprehend much about the births and deaths of her siblings. The tiny coffins were removed from the house before she became aware of them. There was little or no mourning for children under one year old; their deaths were far too common at that time. She played happily with her younger sister, Alice and worshipped her brother, George Henry, as one who could do no wrong. He was a happy-go-lucky child, who seemed to always turn situations to his advantage. Adults liked him, as he was polite and well-behaved; children liked him for his sense of fun. He was very musical, and had been given a harmonica as a Christmas present one year, which he taught himself to play. He would amuse his friends in the street by playing all the popular tunes of the day. When he found that adults also stopped to listen to him, he realised the business potential of his musical prowess, and moved to street corners in the shopping areas, where passers-by would drop him the occasional coin. Consequently George Henry always had a little money of his own, although his father would have been furious had he known, for in George Bolt's eyes, this was tantamount to begging. Harriet said this to George Henry.

'Not so,' said George. 'After all, it's like work. And our Uncle Cornelius and the Sally Army Band play music and collect money for it.'

'Yes,' replied Harriet, 'but they don't keep it for themselves. It goes to God, or the poor or something.'

'Well, at the moment I am poor, but I don't always intend to be.' And George Henry stalked off, head held high.

Sarah continued her work for the tailor, for although George's wages increased steadily, with his enhanced position, he passed most of his money to the local publican. She was as able to make men's clothes as women's. Her children never wore crudely cut-down adult clothes, they were always made-over to fit properly. The Bolts always managed an air of respectability. Harriet, by the age of seven, was proficient at sewing on buttons; she knew they would be tested by the tailor, by twisting and pulling. Her mother had taken her to the tailor's on a number of occasions, to give in the work she had completed. She had seen women in the queue of outworkers having garments thrown back at them, for poor workmanship, and knew that pay depended on quality as well as quantity.

One evening when Sarah was trying to finish a batch of garments for delivery next day, Harriet was staying up late to help. Sarah heard George at the front door.

'Quick, off to bed before your dad comes in!' she said, bundling the sewing into a bag behind the sofa, just as George entered. He knew, but was not supposed to know, that Sarah needed to supplement their income.

'What the hell is going on, woman? What's all this?' He lunged across the room, grabbing Sarah, rather than the sewing. He raised his fist. Harriet, who had been mounting the stairs, turned in horror. Her father's back was towards her. With a cry she jumped on him, grabbing him by the back of his collar.

'Don't you hit my mother, don't you dare beat my mother,' she screamed, hanging on his collar with both hands. George staggered and twisted, but still Harriet clung. His collar began to asphyxiate him. He tried to claw at his collar, as he could not reach the child on his back.

'Get her off me, Sarah, she's choking me,' he gasped. He swung Harriet from side to side, in an effort to free himself. Harriet's grip gave, and she fell to the ground. Sarah rushed to her daughter and faced George defiantly. He yanked at his collar, red in the face with drink, anger and asphyxiation.

'Get out, both of you, get out,' he croaked, pointing at the door. As neither Sarah nor Harriet moved, but stared at him in shock, he lurched menacingly towards them. Sarah grabbed Harriet's hand and they rushed out through the front door, which had remained open since George's entrance. He slammed the door shut and they heard the lock turn.

It was cold, and Harriet's little finger was hurting. She began to cry and held out the injured hand to her mother. Sarah realised that the little finger was sticking out at right-angles to the hand, obviously dislocated. She looked up and down the street.

'What are we going to do, Mother?' Harriet sobbed.

'We will stay the night with Mrs Jessop next door, her husband's on nights, so it will be all right.' Sarah led Harriet to the neighbour's, and knocked at the door. Mrs Jessop answered, in her nightwear with a coat thrown over it. Sarah hated having to parade her ills in front of neighbours, but explained her problem, and showed Harriet's hand. Mrs Jessop was sympathetic, as many women in the street were sufferers of domestic violence. She offered the use of the sofa and an armchair, provided that they would be gone before her husband returned from work in the morning. They made themselves as comfortable as possible, and experienced a fitful night's sleep.

Harriet made a silent, but vehement, vow: 'I will never, never, marry a man who beats me and bruises me. Never!'

There was a covert cameraderie among women, both neighbours and relatives, which was kept from their menfolk. By the time the men came home from work, women were in their respective homes, with the kettle on the hob. No hints were ever made of any help given to others during the day. Money was never lent or borrowed between neighbours, as there was none to spare. There were moneylenders and pawnbrokers for this. When Mrs A__ fell into debt, and pawned her hall rug, she borrowed an identical rug from Mrs. B__. Fortunately one husband was on nightwork, the other days, so the rug was shared for a week. Tangible help and moral support was always forthcoming. Harriet, spending many days off school as her mother's help, absorbed this culture of women without question.

Sarah was awake by dawn, and watching from the window. She saw George leave the house, looking up and down the road, as though expecting to see her and Harriet sleeping in the gutter. His gait was unsteady, but then, it usually was mornings, until he reached the 'Hen and Chicken' for his customary rum and milk before work.

'Old devil,' she muttered under her breath. She watched him set off for work, then woke Harriet.

'Come on,' she said, 'let's get back home and get your brother off to school, and see that Alice is all right. You can go to your own bed and get some rest, then we'll let the doctor see your hand. We'll tell him you did it playing.'

George never mentioned the incident again, but he never forgave Harriet. And Sarah's beatings continued.

Sundays in the Bolt household were different from all other days; for one thing George did not drink on Sundays. He metamorphosed into the ideal Victorian father, strict but fair. The cane still remained on the table at mealtimes, when unsolicited talking from the children was discouraged. Yet he presided over the children's once-a-week bath, in the tin bath in front of the kitchen fire, and helped to wash and dry the girls' hair. He told them stories, of a biblical or moral nature, and sang the occasional hymn, in a rich baritone, for all the Bolts were musical. Although not especially religious, unlike Uncle Cornelius, who belonged to the Salvation Army, and wrote many musical scores for them, George insisted that the Lord's Day should be observed. The children were sent to Sunday School. There were no frivolous songs, no loud games or card games, no playing in the street and no quarreling. Harriet loved Sundays for the peace and tranquility wrought in her father. 'If only he were like this all the time,' she thought.

One Sunday afternoon the children returned from Sunday School; Sarah was laying the table for tea and George was taking a nap on the sofa, next to the table. Taking a hot apple pie from the oven, Sarah placed it carefully on the table.

'Tea time, George, wake up.'

One of George's duties at the sawmills was to order the factory hooter to be blown at the end of the working day. Half-asleep, he associated 'tea-time' with the end of the working day and realising the hooter had not sounded, he raised his fist in the air, shouting 'Blow up, you b*****s!'

To add emphasis he brought his fist crashing down on the table, unfortunately landing in the apple pie, covering him and Sarah in hot apple. Pandemonium broke loose. Harriet and George Henry looked on in horror, then both raced upstairs, trying to stifle their laughter until out of earshot, as the funny side of the situation hit them.

Money was still in short supply, and there would soon be another mouth to feed. Pregnant again, Sarah's time was imminent, and she was trying to complete a final batch of garments for Mr Levy, to insure against the weeks after the birth when she would be unable to take in work. Her labour pains had begun, and there was still the final pressing to be completed, of a number of garments. Sarah had a damp cloth and a bowl of water to hand, to steam the collars flat. Two irons were heating on the stove, to be used alternately as one cooled. During contractions she hung over the ironing table, gasping, and as each contraction finished, she picked up the iron again. George Henry had been dispatched to his aunt's with six-year old Alice; he was then to wait outside the sawmills for his father, to tell him that his mother was 'unwell'. Harriet was waiting for the garments; she was entrusted to take them to Mr Levy's and collect the money due. But the pressing was taking so long!

'Can't I do some?' she asked anxiously, as Sarah paused again, as pain swept over her. Sarah shook her head.

'No, you can't put the pressure on it like I can,' she said, when her breath returned. 'Put your father's dinner to warm in the slow oven; he'll be home early tonight.'

At last the final garment was pressed and all were tied in a neat bundle.

'Now listen,' said Sarah, 'go careful. Don't fall down and get this bundle dirty. Go straight to Mr Levy's. Tell him mother is unwell but will be back soon for more. Wait while he inspects—oh, take a needle and thread in case you need to sew anything there. He should give you one shilling and six pence. Count what he gives you and don't come away from the counter till you're sure it's right.' Sarah paused again, her face contorting as pain washed over her. 'Then come straight back here with the money and put it in the tin.' Sarah kept an old biscuit tin, hidden from George, where her wages and her housekeeping money resided.

Harriet gathered up her bundle.

'Go on now,' urged Sarah. 'I'm alright, and your Grandma will be here soon to help me. Soon you'll have a new little brother or sister.'

'Yes,' thought Harriet, as she kissed her mother, 'and that will be more work.' More and more frequently of late Harriet had been kept home from school to help with the chores, as her mother was busy with sewing, and when pregnant, needed to rest more.

She hurried to the tailor's, where the queue of outworkers had dwindled to nothing, as the women had all returned home to prepare evening meals. She handed over her bundle and gave Sarah's message, then waited as Mr Levy counted out the money. She stood and recounted the money in her hand, as her mother had instructed, then became aware of Mr Levy peering at her over the counter.

'All right?' he asked.

'Yes, thank you,' said Harriet, and turned to go home. By the time she returned her sister, Lily, had been born, her mother was in bed, looking tired but less distressed than when Harriet had left her.

The following week Jack was taken ill, the doctor said it was pneumonia. Sarah's 'lying-in' was prematurely terminated and she found herself tending her new baby and a dying brother. George's mother helped Sarah as much as she could, but she was also ill at the same time with a chest infection. Jack's lungs could not cope and he died in hospital within a few days.

'Most of his life he was no trouble to anybody,' Sarah told Harriet, who was upset at Uncle Jack's death. 'It's a good thing he didn't linger and suffer.'

'I shall miss seeing him sitting by the stove, and I shall miss the stories he told us,' said Harriet. Jack had been one family member who had time to tell a bedtime story to the children—punctuated by coughs.

And I shall miss him and his housekeeping money, thought Sarah. She tackled George the following Sunday. ' Now that Jack has gone I shall not have enough money each week to pay the rent and food bills.'

'Well it's one less mouth to feed,' said George, not intending to be uncaring, just practical. 'Maybe I can find an extra shilling towards the rent, but that's all. After all, I have to live too.'

And so do the brewers, thought Sarah, but she said nothing. A shilling would be a great help.

Lily was a placid baby, spoilt by her two older sisters, and doted on by her elder brother. She never lacked for companionship; when Sarah was busy in the house, Harriet would take Lily out in the pram. She was, by and large, a happy baby, which was why it became so noticeable when she developed 'the grizzles', as Alice called it. During the autumn all the children had contracted colds and coughs which ended in the characteristic 'whoop'. Lily was about nineteen months old, and had suffered a cold and persistent cough for several weeks. Gradually she had become more miserable, the usual distractions failed to amuse her, and her breathing was becoming laboured. Sarah, who was heavily pregnant yet again, took some money from her housekeeping pot and took Lily to see the doctor.

She returned grave-faced. The doctor said that Lily had bronchitis and the cough was whooping cough. Lily had some medicine to take and had to stay in and keep warm. The kitchen was the warmest room, but the coal fire made Lily cough more. Sarah set up a steam kettle to help Lily's breathing, but nothing seemed to aid her recovery.

It was only a few weeks to Christmas when Sarah, trying to cope with extra outwork, Christmas preparations and a sick child, finally came to the end of her tether. She was sitting at the kitchen table, late in the evening, shredding red cabbage for pickling, heaping it into a bowl on the table. Harriet was rocking baby Lily by the fire, George Henry and Alice were in bed, when George came roaring through the front door, drunk as usual. He swayed in front of the table, looking at Sarah, Harriet and Lily, with bloodshot eyes.

'What the bloody hell is going on here?' he shouted, lunging forward at Sarah, as though to strike her.

Something in Sarah snapped. She leapt to her feet and picking up the bowl of shredded red cabbage, threw it at him. Her aim was good, the bowl hit him in the face and the cabbage poured over his entire body. He swayed again, looking at Sarah with her shredding knife still in her hand, then looked down at his chest, which was now covered in red liquid and bits of red cabbage.

'What have you done to me, Sarah?' he moaned. 'You've killed me, for sure.'

'Not this time, George Bolt,' she replied, realising that for once she had the upper hand, due to his drunken incomprehension. 'Go and get those clothes off and go to bed. You can think about this in the morning.'

George did not mention the incident again, and although he continued to drink, he never again attacked Sarah in his drunken rages.

Lily gradually declined, and died two weeks before Christmas, at the age of 20 months. Sarah and George were devastated by her death; they had lost newborn babies in the past, but the loss of a child who was almost two affected them far more. The other children, especially Harriet who had been like a little mother to Lily, were very upset, Christmas would not be a happy time in the Bolt home that year.

Mrs Bolt had been a regular visitor to their home during Lily's illness and after her death. Harriet confided to her grandmother: 'I feel like crying over Lily, but I try not to because it upsets Ma.'

Mrs Bolt hugged her grand-daughter protectively.

'You cry to me, my love. You need to cry, but you are quite right about your mother. You cry to me.'

Harriet buried her face in her grandmother's pinafore and sobbed her heart out. The relief of letting the pent-up tears flow was just what Harriet needed. Eventually she dried her eyes and kissed her grandmother.

'Why did Lily have to die? Uncle Cornelius said she was too good for this world. Does that mean if we are good we will die too?'

'No my love,' Mrs Bolt hid a wry smile. 'She was too ill to get better. These things happen. I don't believe people die because they are too good for this world, or any of that religious stuff. Children die sometimes, especially if you are poor it seems. But you have your mother and father, a brother and a sister, all healthy. And so are you. Just count your blessings.'

Mrs Bolt took Harriet to the corner shop and bought penny sweets for Harriet, George and Alice. That would leave her short of grocery money for her tea. Never mind, she reasoned, the children need this more than I need tea.

At the time of Lily's death, Sarah was expecting twins. Worn down by Lily's illness and death, Sarah struggled through the birth process, producing two living babies, a boy and a girl, William who was born first, then Agnes, a tiny scrap of a girl. After the births, George's mother or one of Sarah's sisters visited each day, to look after Sarah during her lying-in. Harriet, at the age of nine, was in charge of the household at other times.

Taking her mother a cup of tea, the afternoon after the babies had been born, Harriet was surprised to find her mother in tears.

'Something strange has just happened, Harriet,' Sarah explained. 'I think Agnes is not going to be with us for long. I was dozing, and I opened my eyes, and there was someone - an angel I think, with a bright light shining all round her, and she was scattering what looked like rice all round Agnes' cot. She didn't go near William.'

Harriet looked at Agnes; the baby was sleeping peacefully. There was nothing around the cot. 'There's nothing there, mother,' she said. 'You must have dreamed it.'

'No, I saw it. You mark my words, that child has only been lent to us,' Sarah insisted. She told no one else; George would have been very scathing, and the other children would probably have been frightened. Harriet, however, was used to her mother's premonitions, and they were usually right. Just so in this case, baby

Agnes died next day. William grew into a strong, good-looking boy.

Sarah decided to give up her work for the tailor, as George Henry had left school and found a job as a grocer's assistant; he was now bringing home wages. His father was pleased that the boy was not going to be an ignorant labourer, he was using his schooling in writing and money sums.

Harriet left school at twelve, not that she had ever attended often. She viewed leaving school with mixed feelings; one part of her realised how little she had learned at school and how much there was still to know, the rest of her longed to be treated as an adult. Years ago she had left childhood behind; as the eldest daughter her duties and responsibilities were those of an adult, without the status and recognition of adulthood. The only time she was treated as a child was during those hours she spent at school. Now those had come to an end.

She reached home, feeling freed from the mental restrictions of childhood, and went upstairs to the bedroom she shared with Alice. How could she best obtain recognition of her new status? She peered at her reflection in the small mirror, no wrinkles yet. She twirled before the long mirror set in the wardrobe door; she would still have to wear the same clothes, with skirts not quite to her ankles. Her hair! Why had she not thought of that before? She quickly unbraided her childish hairstyle, and with clumsy, unpractised fingers, swept her hair off the nape of her neck and refashioned it into a bun. She used all the hairpins she could find, but they still did not seem enough. Wisps of hair kept detaching themselves from the bun. Never mind, she would improve with practice, and from now on she would wear her hair up so that the world would recognise that she had left school, she was now a grown-up.

In fact little changed for Harriet. It was agreed that she should stay at home to help Sarah, who was pregnant again. Six months later Arthur Stanley was born. Sarah was almost forty years old by then and determined this would be her last child.

George Henry was showing an aptitude for business and learning all that he could, with the idea of one day owning his own shop. Sarah had always hankered after a shop, preferably groceries or greengroceries. George's uncle, Charles, had opened a large greengrocery shop in North Street and was doing well. One day George Henry came home from work saying that his employer, Mrs Hall, wanted to retire, and would like the Bolts to take over her shop in Cabot Street, on the corner of Mill Lane. They would need a deposit as well as the first month's rent and would have to buy the fixtures, fittings and stock. George Henry was very enthusiastic; he felt that he knew the business and the customers, so would be well placed to make a successful takeover. Sarah, too, saw the business potential, and broached the subject with her husband, on his return from work. George, too, was in favour of the move, provided that financial arrangements were satisfactory. By now he was more mature and amenable, and drank less than he had in his youth. His doctor had warned him that he had high blood pressure and should take greater care of his health. He also suffered badly from gout.

George's mother's circumstances had changed; Thomas had died in 1886, leaving her a small amount of money. Mrs Bolt arrived one day and announced that she intended to give up the tenancy of Thomas's house and move to Gloucester, to live with her first husband. George could not believe his ears!

'What?' he roared. 'After leaving you penniless with all us children, you are going back to him as though nothing had ever happened!'

'Forgive and forget, George,' his mother said. 'He needs me, and in a way I suppose, I need him. But he's too ashamed to come back to Bristol to live, so I must go to Gloucester. Anyway, the old devil has offered to keep me for the rest of my life, so I shall not be taking any of Thomas's money with me. If you would like to borrow some to buy the ingoing for the shop then you are welcome.

If I have to come back I shall expect you to house me or return the money.'

The family pooled their resources, gave up their rented house, and with the help of Thomas's legacy took over the shop in 1899, when George Henry was seventeen years old. Mrs Bolt hugged them all, especially Harriet, for whom she had a special fondness, realising how hard the child had worked all her young life.

'I shall come back and see you from time to time,' she said. 'Gloucester is not the other side of the world.'

The family moved into the shop. There was a yard at the back of the premises, with four stables and storage sheds. A pony and cart was purchased, for fetching greengroceries from the market each morning. The other four stables were rented out. Sarah and George Henry were in their element; the business was off the ground. A governess cart was subsequently purchased, so that the family could use it for visiting their relatives on Sundays; George had come close to fulfilling his promise of providing a horse and carriage for Sarah to ride in. Harriet, however, was not so pleased at this latest development. She had always suffered from travel sickness on horse-drawn bus journeys, and found that the governess cart, jolting over the cobbled streets, made her even more nauseous. After several very uncomfortable journeys she begged to be left at home, but George would not allow this. The family travelled as a family, George insisted, although George Henry was often excused visits if he had friends to see or 'business' to attend to.

While the shop was primarily George Henry's responsibility, Sarah and the girls were also involved. Harriet helped in the shop, as she was very quick at reckoning money and soon learned how to look after customers. 'Tea-fish' had become popular; this was salted cod, which was flat and hard, and needed to be soaked overnight. The cod was bought in bulk, and it was Harriet's job to put this in soak Saturday nights and sell it Sunday mornings, for breakfast. However, Harriet, now fourteen years old, had also found herself a job, at Mardon, Son and Hall, a local factory which made cardboard boxes. It gave her improved status in the family, company her own age, a degree of freedom and a little money of her own, for most of her wages were given to her mother each Saturday. From the remainder, Harriet determined to pay for music lessons for herself. George Henry had bought himself a second-hand piano, but Harriet knew she could never emulate her brother. She wondered about singing lessons, as she had a fine contralto voice, but did not know any singing teachers. One of the shop customers, Mrs Davis, was a qualified music teacher, and offered Harriet a second-hand zither and lessons. Harriet was delighted; she was a diligent, able pupil and made great progress.

Harriet began to feel that, at last, she was taking charge of her life. She had a job which provided some money of her own, to pay for her choice of clothes and entertainments. Her status within the family had risen, as she was now paying for her own keep. She had a wider social circle of friends of her own age. The world was still Bedminster-based, but looked less grey to Harriet these days.

HARRIET'S FAMILY

The Bolt Family

Standing: Harriet (born 24 Feb 1885)   Alice (born 1887)
Seated: Mr George Bolt (1859) Arthur (1898) George Henry (1882) William (1894) Mrs Sarah Bolt (1859)
Circa 1903, photo possibly to commemorate George Henry's 21st birthday

Chapter 2

ON GROWING UP

BY THE time Harriet was sixteen, her sister, Alice, was about to leave school, and had also secured a job at Mardon's. She only worked on the factory floor for a few months, before she was offered a post in the office as a clerk. Alice had beautiful handwriting, and was good at figures. 'Well, she had more schooling than me,' Harriet reasoned, pleased for her sister's promotion, but none the less, somewhat envious. The factory work was boring and tedious, although the job was made bearable by the friends she made there.

Alice, once established in her office job, began to affect airs and graces. Sarah made packed lunches for the girls to take to work each day, but Alice refused to carry hers to work, as it would not fit inside the tiny purse she carried. So Harriet carried both lunches to Mardons, passing Alice hers in the canteen at lunchtime. At first Harriet accepted this role but then began to question it and one day she left Alice's lunch on the kitchen table.

Alice walked into the canteen at lunchtime, looking for Harriet, who was quietly eating lunch with some friends.

'Hello Harriet, where's my lunch?' asked Alice.

'At home on the kitchen table,' retorted Harriet. 'If you're too lazy to carry it you will go without in future.'

'Well what shall I eat? It's too far to go home for it, I shall be hungry all afternoon.'

'That's too bad. You have to look after yourself in this grown-up world,' said Harriet evenly, and resumed her conversation with her friends. Alice learned her lesson, dropped her airs and graces and carried her own packed lunch each day.

Harriet had made great progress with her zither lessons, and had taken several exams, passing with high marks. Her music teacher suggested to her that she should make a career of teaching music.

'I'm sure I could get you a place in Cardiff Music School,' she said. 'It would mean you would have to live there in term time. See what your parents think.'

Harriet broached the subject to Sarah and George that evening.

'What!' roared George. 'Have a daughter of mine living away from home! Certainly not! You will live here, my girl, with us, until you get married. Whatever next?'

So Harriet lived at home and continued working in the factory. She was upset, resentful almost, but could see no way of defying her father. If she were to be a student teacher, she would need financial support which could come from no other quarter than her father, so Harriet resigned herself to factory work.

George Henry was making a success of the shop. Early every morning he drove the pony and cart to the fruit and vegetable market, for fresh produce, before he opened the shop. Sarah was always an early riser; she ensured he had a hot breakfast before he started his day's work. George continued working at the sawmills, where he was now a manager, and highly respected. His nightly drinking bouts had ended as he constantly suffered from gout, which caused him so much pain he would not risk the cause. Young William had started school and was proving an able pupil, although he did not show such an aptitude for reading and writing as had George Henry. Arthur was everyone's darling and looking forward to joining his brother at school.

On days when George Henry was not too busy, he would walk to Mardon's, to meet his sisters from work. It gave him an opportunity to mingle with other young men and women his own age; this was how he met Teresa.

'She's the prettiest girl in Mardon's, mother,' George Henry told his mother, his eyes shining.

'Hmm, handsome is as handsome does, George,' Sarah replied. 'You don't court a girl just for her looks, not if you are thinking of a wife.'

But George Henry was smitten and began his courtship of Teresa, which consisted of visits to each other in their parental homes, or meeting on public occasions. When they became engaged, they were able to walk out together arm-in-arm.

Harriet, meanwhile, had met a beau of her own. She had paid scant attention to the approaches of young men, knowing that her father would be furious at any dalliances, and she had never met any young men she wanted to take seriously as a suitor. One Sunday she had taken the tram from Bedminster to Old Market Street, in the centre of the city, to look for some fabric to make a blouse for herself. She was looking in the haberdasher's window, when a voice behind her said 'Excuse me, miss, but can you tell me where the Central Hall is?'

Harriet turned around and looked into the most beautiful pair of brown eyes she had ever seen. Her heart flipped as it had never done before. Recovering her composure with difficulty, she replied, 'Yes, of course. It's just across the road, past The Empire, by the next alleyway.' She pointed at the insignificant building, dwarfed by the elaborate theatre frontage. The young man was about her own age, tall and dark-haired, respectably dressed, as her mother would say, in a jacket, collar and tie. The old Central Hall, at that time, was a converted building where visiting nonconformist ministers preached. It did not proclaim its existence with its name above the door, as its smart 1920s replacement would.

'I am going to hear Mr Symes preach this afternoon,' the young man said. 'Would you care to come with me? He's very well-known and respected.'

Harriet scarcely hesitated. What possible wrong could she be doing, going to church? Even her father would approve—wouldn't he? The young man introduced himself as they crossed the road to the hall. His name was William Fricker, usually called Bill; he was a coal miner and worked at the Dean Lane Pit, in Bedminster, as did his father.

There were three coal mines in Bedminster at that time, Dean Lane Pit, Malago Vale Pit and South Liberty, which bordered Bedminster Down. Mining was recognised as dangerous and arduous, and the miners had been active in forming workers coalitions which became the basis of a nationally recognised union before the end of the century. This gave some guidelines for safety, but wages were negotiated regionally. The poor quality and quantity of Bristol coal was given as the reason for their miners being paid one fifth less than the national average but much of Bristol's coal was used to fire Bristol's industries so transport costs were minimal.

'Do you have any brothers or sisters?' Harriet asked, and was amazed at the way William laughed.

'Dozens of them!' He reeled off a list of names, then added, 'some of those are only half-brothers and sisters, as my mother died and father married again.' Harriet was not surprised at this. When the mother of a family died, the best thing a father could do, to keep his family together, was to marry again without delay.

'Do you get on well with your stepmother?' she asked.

'She is a wonderful woman,' Bill replied, 'She is kindness itself. I think of her as my mother, as I was only two when my own mother died.'

Harriet enjoyed her afternoon spent with Bill. He asked if he could see her the following weekend. Harriet agreed, knowing that she would first have to tell her parents about Bill.

'You met him where?' her father asked, frowning. His son could have free rein, but his daughters had to be controlled, chaperoned and protected.

'At the Central Hall, father, Mary Onion and I went to hear the new preacher there.' A little white lie wouldn't hurt, Harriet reasoned.

'And what job does he have?'

'He's a miner, father, as his father and brother.'

George Bolt considered these two pieces of information together. Miners tended to fall into two categories, those who were wild, lawless men or those who were God-fearing. The latter tended to be Baptists, or other non-conformist denominations, due to the work of Wesley and other religious reformers, who had targeted the unrestrained miners in the previous century. Those preachers had seen it as their duty to save the souls of the wild, hard-drinking men who toiled underground, and give them Sunday as a day off work, in order to praise their Maker, much to the chagrin of the mine owners. Obviously this young man Harriet had met was the religious type, which George would prefer for his daughter, provided he was not too extreme. George's Uncle William and Uncle Cornelius still worked in Bristol mines, both were God-fearing men though William was not a great church-goer nowadays; Uncle Cornelius and his son were both miners and Salvationists. However, his father's uncle and a cousin had both been killed in separate pit accidents and his grandfather had gone blind through eye infections due to coal dust. George and his own father had always avoided mining as a job, as it was known to be highly dangerous—and besides, who wanted to spend ten hours a day working in the dark, with only a candle's light for company?

Harriet waited, watching her father think. To interrupt him would mean instant dismissal of her case. Eventually he said 'When the young man calls for you next weekend, I would like to meet him, before you go anywhere.'

Harriet realised this was Bill on trial, one false move and her father would refuse to let her see him again; it was not as though her father already knew Bill or his family, which would have provided some background information for his assessment.

When Bill arrived the following week, he looked smart, wearing a dark jacket over a clean shirt, collar and tie. Harriet could tell her father approved of his appearance. He asked Bill a number of questions about his job, his family and his opinions of the world. On the latter Bill was reticent, saying that he was too young to have formulated decisive opinions as yet; he was only seventeen, the same age as Harriet. His answers seemed to satisfy George, who gave them permission to go out for the afternoon together.

A few weeks later Harriet met Bill's father and stepmother, together with the numerous brothers and sisters who still lived at home; Harriet wondered how they all crammed into one small terraced house, but they all seemed happy together. She understood why Bill was so fond of his stepmother; Martha Fricker was a kind and generous woman who managed the large household good-humouredly, always finding time to talk to individual children, making them feel that their problems were important but could be solved with her help. The family attended the Chapel opposite their house in Sion Road, Bedminster, and Harriet joined them there on many occasions.

A long courtship ensued; they could only meet at weekends due to the long hours Bill worked, but they both realised they were falling in love. On Harriet's eighteenth birthday Bill gave her a brooch.

'I hope you like it, Harriet,' he said, 'I would like to have given you more, but it is all I could afford. I would like to have offered you a ring; I'm sure you know I want to marry you, but I don't think your father would agree as yet. Perhaps you will wear this brooch as our own private promise?'

Harriet took the brooch and kissed Bill on the cheek, her heart thumping. 'I would love to, Bill. You know there's no one else in my life but you.'

Eventually Bill asked George if he might become engaged to his daughter. George made much of the paucity of Bill's job, lack of income, no job promotion, danger, long hours, but gave his permission.

'But I'll say the same to you, Harriet, as I've said to my son, you will not get married until you are twenty-one. Your mother and I were twenty-one when we got married; by then you are old enough to know your own minds, you are adults and can make your own mistakes. That way you can't come back to me complaining that I let you get married too young.' George was thinking of two of his sisters, who had married young and regretted it within a few years; also Sarah's sister, Harriet, who married dashing young Martin when only eighteen and then spent most of her married life alone whilst he was in jail. George did not want any scandal or disasters within his own family

Bill gave Harriet an inexpensive ring and they were now able to walk down the road arm-in-arm. It would be a long engagement while they both tried to save for their marriage. Harriet spent her weekday evenings sewing, embroidering and crocheting items for her 'bottom drawer'. This was literally the large drawer at the bottom of the chest in the bedroom she shared with Alice, which she began to fill with linens she would need for married life. She and Bill tried to save money from their meagre salaries; Bill less successfully as he came from such a large family and there was always someone who needed something. Harriet decided to economise by giving up her much-loved music lessons, although she still played her zither.

Harriet was envious when George Henry announced one day, 'Teresa and I are getting married on Boxing Day.' He would be twenty-one and one month. The wedding was to take place at the local Anglican church, St John's, although Teresa was Catholic. There was one concession Teresa would not make, however, she refused adamantly to move into the shop. The reason she gave was that she did not see herself living over a shop; in addition, she did not see herself living with George Henry's parents. They found a house, in Phillip Street, and Teresa's mother, who was a widow, moved in with them shortly after the wedding.

Teresa started married life as she meant to continue; there was to be no rising early to cook George Henry a breakfast before he went to the fruit market each morning. Her mother was living with them, and could therefore pay her way by doing the housework, leaving Teresa nothing to do but look after herself and read her penny-novels. Harriet watched the scenario in amazement; she thought that Teresa was the laziest woman she had ever encountered. Sarah worried about her son, completing a morning's work without his accustomed good breakfast; from time to time she cooked him bacon and eggs on his return from market, if the shop was quiet and he had time to eat. But Sarah was not in good health, and could not be expected to shoulder the type of workload she had in the past. She was suffering increasingly from shortness of breath, which she had always attributed to inhaling the dressing in the fabrics she had sewn, in the past. Although she was no longer sewing, her breathing had never recovered, in fact as she grew older, it seemed to deteriorate.

The seeds of discontent had been sown; within six months of the wedding Sarah, George and George Henry had decided to relinquish the shop. George Henry found a junior management position at one of the Bristol Breweries—coincidentally named George's Brewery. Sarah and George and their four remaining children, Harriet, Alice, William and Arthur, began looking for a house to buy. The local agent took them to see a large double-bayed house, which appeared to be very comodious for the price asked. He showed them around the house, which seemed more than adequate. But when he took them into the front parlour, Sarah almost fainted. She pulled at the neck of her clothes, gasping 'George, get me out of here. I can't breathe.'

'Whatever is wrong with you, woman?' George retorted brusquely, but his wife's distress was so real that he almost carried her from the house. The agent followed them, pale of face.

'I'm sorry, Mr Bolt,' the man said. 'Is your wife a clairvoyant or something?'

'Don't be stupid, man, whatever do you mean?'

'Well –' the man hesitated, then confessed, 'the last occupant hanged herself in that room.'

George was furious that the man had shown them the house without warning them in advance. A change of agent produced a suitable property and the family moved to a house in Fairfield

Terrace, on Whitehouse Lane. George's mother returned from Gloucester, as Mr Bolt had died, and George rented her a house opposite the family home; Harriet moved in with her grandmother as companion. Old Mrs Bolt was delighted to meet Harriet's fiance, inviting him for Sunday tea before they went for a walk one Sunday evening.

'What did you think of him, Grandma?' asked Harriet, on her return. She had become increasingly fond of the old lady since moving to stay with her and hoped for a favourable opinion.

'I think he is a steady young man, polite and very fond of you Harriet, as you are of him. I don't see why your father doesn't let you get married, it's obviously going to last.' Harriet smiled at her grandmother's approval.

Alice had met a young man, Jim Budd, and fallen in love. Unfortunately he did not strike a good impression with George Bolt, when they met for the first time; he had the temerity to wear a kerchief knotted round his neck, instead of a collar and tie. George had also heard some detrimental rumours about Jim's past behaviour, he had been a 'bit of a tearaway' when younger. Alice, as always a very determined young woman, was convinced she could wear her father's resistance down. Jim, once he had met Alice, behaved impeccably and George gradually accepted him as Alice's beau.

The love between Harriet and Bill continued to flourish. They still only met at weekends, but over the years Harriet became acquainted with his numerous brothers and sisters. She became especially fond of Ellen, who was a few years older than Harriet, a plump, smiling girl, with a happy outgoing nature. One weekend Harriet sensed there was tension and friction in the Fricker household. When she and Bill went for a walk together, he explained.

'Ellen is in the family way,' he said directly, 'it's her employer's child.' Ellen had been in service since she left school; she currently worked for a farmer and his wife, as a housemaid and dairymaid. The dairy had been the site of Ellen's downfall. However, the man had admitted his responsibility and was arranging for the baby to be taken and fostered at his expense. Ellen would have preferred to look after the baby herself, but this was out of the question, because then she would have no job and no income. Mr and Mrs Fricker were devastated, not just because of Ellen's misdemeanor, but that they had neither the money nor the space to offer Ellen and her child a home.

Harriet called to see Ellen at Bill's home the following evening on her way home from work. Ellen had been given two days off from the farm, in order to visit her family.

'However did this happen, Ellen? Is there nothing to be done?'

Ellen's round apple-cheeks were drawn and tearstained. 'He caught me in the corner of the dairy, by the milk cooler. He's very persuasive and forceful. I never thought about a baby.' Tears began again. 'I don't want to give my child over to someone else but I can't afford to keep him, I've got to work. If I don't, the only choice is the Workhouse, and I can't face that for the rest of my life.'

Harriet was very upset at the feelings of helplessness overwhelming Ellen; her fate was being decided for her. Emotional bonds had to be secondary to the need to make a living. She tried to comfort her friend, but found there was little she could say. When Bill returned from work he walked her home; both were in a sober frame of mind and exchanged few words.

Four months later Ellen's baby was born at Snowdon Buildings, a boy whom she named Reginald after his father, was placed with his fosterparents and Ellen returned to work at the farm. The farmer's wife, who was a semi-invalid and retired to bed each afternoon, had decided to ignore the whole incident; after all Ellen was a good worker. Her husband's indiscretions had to be overlooked, as it saved her bothering with that side of married life any longer. Ellen went to visit her son as often as she could, taking him little presents. They were a kindly couple, the fosterparents, but it was still a tremendous wrench for Ellen each time she left her son, with the prospect of not being able to see him again for another few weeks. Harriet saw less of her, as Ellen's meagre time off from work, two half-days a month, were usually spent visiting her son.

By the time Harriet and Bill were twenty they were looking for a place of their own to set up in married life. One weekend Bill called to collect Harriet, in great excitement; he had found two affordable rooms to rent, not far from his family home. Harriet went to view the little terraced house, and they agreed it was ideal. They then had to persuade her father that the marriage should take place; they both returned to Harriet's home to speak to him.

'Mr Bolt,' Bill began, 'I remember you saying that Harriet should not get married until she was twenty-one. Well, she's almost that now, and we have been very constant to each other for a number of years.' He began to stumble slightly. 'Well, the fact is, there are some rooms to let in a house just up the road from my father's house, which I could afford on my money. Could I speak for them and Harriet and I get married and move in?'

George's frown had begun to deepen as Bill spoke.

'You can rent as many rooms as you like, young man. I can't forbid you that. But why should I change my mind about my daughter getting married before she's twenty-one? Have your prospects changed? Is there a new situation I don't know about?'

'Well no, sir, except if we miss these rooms, we might not get anything else so cheap or convenient to my work,' Bill replied, feeling that he was losing ground. Harriet stood beside him, not knowing whether to add anything, or whether her intervention would only anger her father. To everyone's amazement the usually acquiescent Sarah, who was standing in the doorway stepped in, for once.

'George, it is only a few months to Harriet's twenty-first birthday. If they lose the chance of this accommodation they might not find anything else so reasonable and then we should feel duty bound to offer them to live with us, just as your mother and Mr Jupe did when we first got married.'

It was obvious from George Bolt's expression he had not considered this. He remembered his mother and Mr Jupe putting up with overcrowding, and a young baby, and he shuddered at the thought of his quiet domicile being disrupted so.

'Well, things might not come to that,' he blustered. 'When are you twenty-one, Harriet?'

'February, father.'

George thought for a moment. 'Very well,' he said, 'I give my permission. Rent your rooms and organise your wedding.'

Harriet and her mother clapped and cried, George and Bill shook hands, and Bill rushed off to tell his parents, who had been unable to see why there was any delay for so many years.

Alice was overjoyed at her sister's forthcoming wedding. 'Can I be bridesmaid to you, Harriet, please?' she begged.

'Well, I hadn't thought about a fancy wedding,' Harriet mused, 'Bill and I don't plan to spend much on the wedding, I don't know about father.'

'I'll buy my own dress if father won't, and I planned to get some new shoes in the spring, so I'll only be getting them a month early.'

The wedding took place in early January at St John's Church, Bedminster; Harriet wore a blue dress, which would serve very well as a 'best' dress later on. Only those with money to burn were married in white; what would you do with a white dress afterwards, Harriet wondered. Alice was not only bridesmaid but signed the register as one of the witnesses, along with Harriet's father. Mr and Mrs Fricker demured, saying that they did not write well enough. Harriet gladly gave up her job at Mardon's, as few young married women went out to work; those who needed extra income had to take in work, but no-one started married life that way.

She became integrated into Bill's extended family easily. His stepmother and father were kind, loving people, with enough warmth to encompass their own numerous children and their spouses. Bill's stepmother, Mr Fricker's third wife, took to Harriet like a daughter. Harriet was pleased to have a home of her own, housekeeping came easily to her, and she was able to manage well on Bill's money. What she was not prepared for was that a miner came home from work black from top to toe each day. She was also shocked when Bill stripped off his shirt to wash, that his back was covered with sores and boils.

'The coal seams in this pit are narrow,' Bill explained, 'so the tunnels where we work are very low. The men all work without shirts as it gets hot underground so our backs become continually scratched and infected.' Harriet bathed his sores as he sat in the tin bath in the kitchen and applied ointment, in a constant battle to lessen the infection.

Within a few months of their wedding Harriet became pregnant; both she and Bill were delighted. They had not told any of their respective families, hugging their secret to themselves but Bill inadvertently gave the secret away. He had started feeling nauseous during the early mornings; one day, on his way to the mine with his father for the early shift he had to turn aside and be sick at the side of the road. His father regarded him with an amused smile.

'Harriet in the family way, is she?' he asked, when Bill regained his composure. 'I always used to be sick when your mother was in the family way. Saved her having to do that bit of the childbearing. Don't find I have to do that with Martha though.' His eyes twinkled, and he walked on.

Bill was always a solicitous husband, Harriet thought, not a bit like her own father. Obviously he had taken the pattern from his father, who was always kind and caring, and took more of the childcare than most Victorian fathers. During her pregnancy, Bill was even more attentive. On Sundays, his day off from work, he would help with the heavier housework. One day he was on his hands and knees, polishing the linoleum in the hallway, when one of his friends called.

'Hello Bill, what you doing? Is Harriet ill?' the man asked.

'No, she's very well, Joe, and while I can keep her well, I will,' Bill replied. 'What can I do for you?'

Alice Mabel was born in the first week of July; she was called

Alice after Harriet's sister and Mabel for one of Bill's sisters, so both families were content. Harriet remembered her mother's exhaustion after childbirth, but hers seemed to get worse the next day, not ease. She began to run a temperature and Mrs Fricker, who had seen other women die of post-natal fever, sent for Harriet's mother early that morning. Sarah, too, was worried and called their family doctor. He examined Harriet carefully and enquired about her symptoms. He gave Harriet medicine to lower her temperature and help fight off the infection, and promised to call next day.

The next day Harriet was no better, in fact, she felt worse, as now all her joints were aching. She could scarcely hold a cup; rocking the cradle was beyond her. The doctor returned a diagnosis of rheumatic fever and forecast it would be some weeks before Harriet recovered. He warned that she might be left with some weakness.

Bill was frantic with worry, but had to leave Harriet at home while he went to work. No work meant no pay for a miner, whatever the circumstances. His stepmother and Harriet's mother took turns at looking after Harriet and the new baby by day. Alice, who was very worried about her sister's illness, called in after work each day for an hour and Bill took over as soon as he returned from work. Bill's sisters and his brother's wife Saranne all took turns at helping as best they could. Gradually Harriet's strength began to return; by the end of a month she was able to walk around her bedroom, the following week tackling the stairs, and eventually taking over her own household duties. Baby Alice seemed none the worse for the calamitous start to her life, and continued to thrive.

There was some friction at the mine, Harriet knew, although Bill had not said a great deal about it. Dean Lane Pit had not had a very good safety record, and the Frickers were very safety conscious. George, Bill's elder brother, was talking about changing to Easton Pit. Bill's father was in favour of moving back to Somerset, where the family had originated, and working at one of the Waldegrave mines. She broached the subject with Mrs Fricker.

'Bill's father moves house for a pastime,' she said to Harriet. 'When I met him first he was living at Bedminster Down, working the Pit there. Then Hannah, his first wife died in childbirth and he moved to Bristol. He was only married to his second wife a year and she died giving birth to young Gilbert. When William and I married we moved to here, as it was a bigger house and we had more room for the kiddies. But he and Hannah and the first four or five of their children were all born in Timsbury; I think he wants to go back, the trouble at the pit is just the last straw. He went to Somerset last Sunday, to enquire about jobs and housing.'

It came as no surprise to the two women that a few weeks later Mr Fricker announced that the family would be moving to Somerset, to Peasedown St John, where he had been offered a miner's cottage to go with the job at the mine. He wanted his sons to move with him, but George pointed out that he had only just started at Easton Pit, and besides, his wife Saranne was a city girl and did not relish the idea of country life.

'How about you, Harriet?' Bill asked, cautiously. 'It would be good for our children to be brought up in the country, breathing in clean air. It sounds as though the miners are well looked after there and we would have a cottage of our own.'

That was the great incentive for Harriet, who agreed, and the three of them moved to Peasedown St John in late September, in time to enjoy the spectacular colours of autumn in the countryside. Their cottage had a living-room with a small range, and a scullery at the back, with two bedrooms upstairs. Harriet, who had always been a city girl, was surprised how easily she adapted to country living, although she missed her constant contact with her mother and sister. Mrs Fricker was delighted to have Harriet back as her neighbour once again, and introduced her to other miners' wives. The miners' cottages were grouped together, and the wives formed a strong community. It seemed strange to go to the communal pump for water, as none was piped to individual houses. There was an outside privy at the back of each cottage. Some of the men dug holes in field hedgerows and buried the contents of the privy buckets, but Harriet and Mrs Fricker paid Mr Withers two pence a week to remove the contents.

'What does he do with it?' Harriet asked Mrs Fricker.

'I don't know for sure, but he has a market garden; I think he might use it there. They say he grows lovely vegetables.' Harriet wrinkled her nose and made a mental note not to buy vegetables from Mr Withers.

The year after Alice Mabel was born, the Frickers were stunned by a revelation from Ellen that she was pregnant again. The farmer had once again cornered her in the dairy one afternoon, and forced himself on her. Ellen was devastated when she realised she was pregnant again, even more as this time he refused to take any responsibility for his actions, and tried to claim that Ellen had other young men. But he had reckoned without Ellen's determination. She took him to court, a long and painful ordeal, especially with the legislation of the time, suffered the snide unpleasantries of the presiding magistrates, and won her case. The farmer was ordered to pay for the maintenance of the child until he was of an age to go to work. Ellen called the baby William, after her own father, and placed him with the couple who fostered her first child, so that the two brothers should be together. She set about finding herself a new job, which was not easy without an employer's reference.

As Harriet cuddled Alice Mabel, she wept a few tears for Ellen. She may have won her battle, but she still did not have her sons. She herself felt so secure in Bill's love, and happy with her child, that she wished everyone could experience the same. Once a month or so she took the train to Bedminster, to visit her mother and other relatives. When she was in Peasedown she felt that Bill's mother was almost like a mother to her.

By the time Alice Mabel was two, Harriet was expecting another baby. One cold November morning Harriet was astounded to open her cottage door to see Alice trudging down the lane towards her.

'Alice, what are you doing here? How lovely to see you,' Harriet cried, opening her arms to her sister, then noticing Alice's straight face, with not a glimmer of a smile.

'Let's go inside Harriet.' Alice shut the door behind them. 'Our mother said I was to take the day off work and come and let you know that grandma died yesterday. She thought you'd want to know as the funeral is on Sunday. Oh—goodness, Harriet, do sit down, you've gone all white.'

Alice was right, the news had shocked Harriet; she had not seen her grandmother for a while as she had discontinued her regular visits to Bedminster due to her pregnancy.

'What was wrong with her, Alice? She seemed so well last time I saw her.'

'She went down with a cold some weeks back and developed pneumonia the doctor said. Mother thought she was getting better, so she didn't send for you, then suddenly she went downhill and passed away within twenty-four hours. Father is distraught, I never realised he was so fond of grandma,' Alice said.

'Well it was his mother, after all, Alice. Make us a cup of tea, the kettle's on the hob.'

Bill and Harriet attended the funeral the following Sunday, leaving little Alice Mabel with Bill's family. Harriet wept as the funeral cortege followed the coffin to Arnos Vale cemetery, thinking of the kindly grandmother she had loved so much.

The following month, with Harriet heavily pregnant, they decided to visit Harriet's parents and siblings in Bristol, as Bill had two days off work for Christmas. They stayed with Bill's brother, George, who still lived and worked at the Easton Pit and his wife, Saranne. On Boxing Day Harriet went into labour. Bill was due to return to Peasedown for work the next morning.

'I can't go, Harriet,' he said, visibly upset, 'I shall just lose a day's pay.'

'You better go, Bill,' Harriet urged. 'It's pay that we can't afford to lose and you might even lose your job.' Employers still regarded childbirth as 'women's work'; their menfolk were not expected to take time off for such events. 'I shall be all right here with Saranne and George. My mother's nearby and will come for the birth, I'm sure. The second birth is nowhere near as difficult as the first, I shall be fine. Come back on Sunday and you will see your new baby.'

Bill would not hear of it, and the following day Lilian Gladys was born, and was named Lilian after Harriet's sister who had died in infancy and Gladys after Bill's youngest sister. Bill was delighted with his new daughter whom he pronounced well worth the wait. Harriet knew he would have liked a boy, as would she, but he seemed very content with another daughter, saying that the two girls would be company for each other.

Harriet and the two children stayed with George and Saranne until Harriet was fit enough to make the journey home a few weeks later. Harriet was pleased that Lilian had been born in Bristol; had anything gone wrong during the birth she would have received better medical attention in the city, she reasoned. Also it was easier for her mother and other relatives to see the baby. Harriet had missed her mother, as the two of them had always been very close; although she enjoyed living at Peasedown, she was too distant for frequent family visits.

Sarah was delighted with her new grandaughter, and visited Harriet every day while they were in Bristol. Harriet's sister, Alice, also visited, to see her new niece and to give Harriet her news, that she was to be married to Jim in a few months time. At last, thought Harriet, although she did not like Jim much, after all, Alice is twenty-three; most girls are married long before that age. The courtship had been prolonged because their father, George Bolt, viewed Jim and his family as rough and not good enough for his daughter. He kept hoping that Alice would meet someone 'more suitable'; after all, the Bolts were now a family of some standing. They had owned a substantial grocery and green-grocery shop, George Henry now had a white-collar job, while George senior was a well-respected manager at the sawmills. But Alice and Jim had proved their constancy, and Jim his good behaviour, so they were to be married in the spring of 1910.

Alice was so full of her news and plans, she was completely unaware of her namesake, little Alice, now age three, eyeing the packet of biscuits protruding from her shopping bag. The child was too well-mannered to ask for one. Harriet was sure that her sister would give her the pack of biscuits as a present when she left, but no, the biscuits went home in Alice's bag. Typical, thought Harriet, not even one for little Alice, just doesn't think.

The following Sunday, Bill returned to take Harriet and the children home to Peasedown, by train from Temple Meads. They waved goodbye to Bill's brother, George, and Saranne.

Over the Christmas break George had been telling Bill about the recent mine expansion at Hanham, on the outskirts of Bristol. They were taking on more miners, he said, prospects might be good there. The old shallow seams at the Easton Pit, and in fact most of the Bristol pits, were practically exhausted now. Men had to walk almost two miles in some areas, before they reached the coalface.

'In fact,' George said, 'the Dean Lane tunnels have almost met up with the Easton tunnels underground. Whereas, while there have been mines in the Hanham and Kingswood areas for hundreds of years, the opening of a new vein sounds promising. I am having to work very hard to make a living with the poor seams at Easton so I am thinking of trying my luck at Hanham.' Bill was interested in the prospect and resolved to discuss it with his father.

Within six months George Fricker had secured himself a job and a miner's cottage at the Hanham mine. Bill and his father visited the area and they, too, found jobs and adjacent cottages available for rent in Footshill, a little farther from the pit. Harriet and Mrs Fricker discussed their impending move to Hanham; neither had seen the cottages where they were to live.

Mrs Fricker said to Harriet, 'I told you, he moves house for a pastime, never consults anyone, just ups sticks and we all have to go.'

'I'm quite happy to move to Hanham. It sounds nice and I shall be nearer to my family in Bedminster, because they have just extended the tram service from Bristol as far as Hanham. Bill said there's also piped water to the cottages, which will make life with two small children much easier.'

The two cottages rented by Bill and his father were in a rank of four, in Footshill, at the commencement of the rise leading out of the village. To reach the mine, half a mile away, the men would have to walk down the hill, past the public house, called The Crown and Horseshoe, and the rank of miners' cottages where Bill's brother, George, lived with his family. The entrance to the mine, flanked by two grey stone pillars, was on the right hand side of the road. The men soon settled in to the routine of the new mine; the brothers frequently worked on the same shifts. Harriet was very happy in her new home—the third in as many years.

The cottages were built of grey stone, with tiny walled front gardens, and a front gate for each. The front door opened into a narrow passageway, with a door on the left leading to the front parlour, at the rear was the living room, with a range for cooking. The stairs led from this room to an open landing, which would serve as a bedroom for the two girls; the front bedroom was for Harriet and Bill. Behind the living room there was a small scullery, with a copper boiler in the corner and a tin bath hanging on the wall. At the back of each cottage was a small cobbled yard, with a brick-built shed which housed the lavatory.

Harriet set about making the cottage as homely and comfortable as her frugal budget would allow. She still had her stock of linens from her bottom drawer; she made single sheets for the children's beds from worn sheets from her double bed. She crocheted new mantle covers for the fireplaces in both rooms, and chairback covers for Bill's easy chair.

Although Hanham was more accessible to Bristol, it was still surrounded by rolling countryside. On Sundays when the weather was fine, Harriet and Bill would take the children to Hanham Mills for a picnic, little Lilian riding on Bill's shoulders. Sometimes they stopped by the river, and Bill bought them all a lemonade each. Harriet thought she could never be so happy, and confided to Bill that she thought she might be pregnant again. Each secretly hoped it would be a boy this time.

HARRIET'S FAMILY

Harriet and William (Bill) Fricker
Circa 1906, possibly to commemorate their wedding. Harriet's corseted waist measured 18 inches; Bill's hands could encircle her waist.

Chapter 3

THE PRICE WE PAY FOR COAL

APRIL 27TH 1911 was a crisp, fine day, but with enough nip in the air to remind everyone that this was still early Spring. Harriet held Lilian's hand, as the toddler walked along the top of the front wall outside of the cottage. Alice, nearly five, re-arranged her dolls in their pram, inside the four-foot strip they called the front garden. Bill's shift at the pit had begun at seven in the morning and sometimes he came home for his lunch break, as the South Side seam where he was working was not far from home. Harriet always liked to be at the gate to see him coming up the road; her heart still skipped a beat at the sight of him. Her free hand slid unconsciously to her stayed waistline; a few more weeks and her stays would be let out a little. Please let it be a boy this time, she prayed. They loved both of their girls, but each knew that the other longed for a son. They had not planned to have another child so soon, as money was not plentiful. But still, she was a good manager, and Bill a good worker. They would be fine, as long as the mine was steady.

Four weeks ago the canary had been carried from the pit, dead, so the men had refused to work for several days until the suspected gas had cleared. The pit had been re-ventilated as the pit owners were anxious for the miners to return to work. Safety lamps were also to be installed throughout, but as yet this work was not completed. Many of the men still worked by the light of naked candles, although this was considered bad practice by more advanced mines. Two days ago one of the other inspectors had detected gas, but very little, so the men were instructed to continue working.

Suddenly the air was rent with the shrill cry of the pit hooter. Instead of simply signalling the end of the shift, with a short double burst, its cry continued on, making Harriet want to cover her ears. Lilian's face crumpled, and she began to cry, so Harriet scooped her into her arms and hugged her close. Bill's father ran from his cottage next door, dragging on his jacket. Other men came running along the road, towards the mine, faces grim-set.

'Whatever is it, Mr Fricker?' called Harriet.

'Something wrong at the pit,' he replied. 'Go inside, girl, I'll find out. Our George is down there - is Bill?'

'Yes—oh, do hurry!' An icy wave crept through Harriet's body. Alice was tugging at her skirt, demanding to know what was happening, as Bill's stepmother emerged from her cottage, wiping floury hands on her apron.

'Did you say Bill's at the pit, as well as our George?' she asked.

'Yes, they're on the same shift now. I want to go and see what's happened. Can I leave the children with you?'

'If you feel you should,' she replied.

'Oh please, Mrs Fricker.' Harriet passed Lilian to her mother-in-law, and helped Alice next door with her dolls' pram. 'I'll be back as soon as I know Bill's all right.'

Harriet half-ran the mile to the pit gates. She headed for the cluster of people near one of the mine shafts. 'What is it?' she asked of no one in particular. One or two of the heads turned towards her. 'Explosion below ground' someone said. The words echoed round Harriet's head, as though in a void; did she understand these words? What did they mean? What were the implications? Men and women were standing in grim silence, with lowered heads, occasionally there was a whisper between a small group of people, then silence again, as though they were listening for any information which might be forthcoming.

She scanned the crowd; there was no sign of her father-in-law. She saw one of his friends who ran the employees' sick club. She clutched his arm.

'Is anyone hurt? Where's Bill? He was on this shift.'

'I don't know yet, Mrs Fricker, they are bringing men out now. Now, wouldn't you be better at home? There's nothing you can do here.' He hurried away, not waiting for her reply. She stared at his receding back, and the icy emptiness returned.

A few emerging miners, with blackened, streaked faces, and eyes white and wide with terror, were surrounded by friends, relatives and pit officials, all wanting to know details of what had happened. Harriet made her way towards the crowd. Bill was not there, neither was George, his brother.

'Did anyone see Bill Fricker?' she asked. 'Please, did anyone see Bill Fricker?'

'We couldn't see anything, missus. Smoke and dust.' 'There's more men on their way out,' another voice added. 'The rescue team's gone in.'

Harriet's legs began to buckle, and she hastily looked around for somewhere to sit, before she fell down. There was a heap of large stones near the pithead, and she perched on them. One of the women from the crowd, a Mrs Hooper, whom Harriet knew by sight, came to talk to her; saying that her husband, too, was below ground. Harriet answered her mechanically, not taking in anything the woman was saying. She looked around for George's wife, Saranne, then remembered that she had gone to visit her mother that day.

The crowd began to thin. The miners went into the pit office, to give their accounts to the duty manager; their relatives waited at the door. Other men from the rescue team descended the shaft. A man emerged from the pit office and jumped on a bicycle, cycling away fast. One of those waiting outside the pit office crossed to the others at the pithead.

'He's gone for transport,' he said. 'Seems there's some injured down there who will need to go to hospital.'

'Oh God, not Bill, please not Bill,' Harriet prayed silently. She looked at the people still waiting with her, at the pithead, knowing that each was also silently offering his or her own prayer. Murmurings began among the remaining crowd; conjectures and theories, blame and absolutions passed back and forth, around Harriet's head, like children's games of shuttlecock. She felt herself no part of this, as though she was watching a dream, but not participating.

Suddenly there was a flurry of activity around the pithead. Bill, George, George Hooper and another man, whom Harriet did not recognise, were being half-carried out of the pit entrance by Bill's father and the rescue team.

Harriet ran forward as the men were taken into the pit office for first aid to their burns, oil and cotton-wool. Bill was barely conscious, his face and body were blackened and scorched, his hands and arms were very badly burned; he was also having some difficulty breathing.

'It's the blast, missus, knocks the air out of you,' explained one of the rescue team.

Harriet managed to speak to Bill before a car arrived to take the men to Cossham Hospital. 'I will come and see you tomorrow,' Harriet wept, 'I'm sure your ma will have the girls.'

That night Harriet lost the baby she was carrying. When the bleeding began, her daughters were in bed; she was able to call Bill's stepmother from their cottage next door.

'How far on were you?' she asked.

'Only about six or seven weeks,' Harriet replied. 'I wasn't really sure I was pregnant.'

'Well, you're not now, and you've got enough to think about without that, so try to get some sleep and tomorrow I'll have the girls and you can go to the hospital to see Bill if you're well enough,' Mrs Fricker said, not unkindly. She tucked Harriet into bed, then let herself out of the cottage. Harriet shed a few tears, silently, some for the lost baby, some for Bill and some for herself. At twenty-six she felt she was shouldering a heavy load.

The next day Harriet and Saranne went to see Bill and George in hospital. Bill's hands and arms were swathed in bandages. His entire body had been burnt, some areas more deeply than others. He was drifting in and out of consciousness, hardly able to speak.

During one of his brief periods of consciousness, Bill recognised her. 'You . . . . all right?' he managed to gasp. Harriet realised he was trying to determine whether or not she was pregnant; he had been worried about how they would manage. Now things would have been even more difficult.

'I'm not having a baby,' she told him. 'I started last night.'

Bill sighed, his eyes closed again.

'He has a lot of willpower, Mrs Fricker, we are doing all we can. You must hope and pray,' the hospital staff told her.

The doctor, however, was more forthright. 'If he recovers, Mrs Fricker, he will never have the use of his hands again. They are burned like two drumsticks. I suppose he was carrying one of the candles which ignited the gas.'

For two more days Bill battled desperately to hang on to life, but finally gave up the struggle on April 30th 1911. George Hooper survived until May 8th. He was forty-two years old and left a wife and four children. Bill's brother, George, and Frederick Hooper, the other miners directly involved in the accident, were ill for several months but both made a full recovery.

Bill's funeral was arranged for the following Sunday, so that miners from Hanham Colliery could attend without losing a day's pay. Mines were always closed on the day that any miner was killed at work as a mark of respect. Even then, the miners lost the remainder of that day's pay; it was an unusual mine owner who paid full wages during closure, for whatever reason. Harriet's and Bill's other relatives would also be able to come to the funeral without losing a day's pay.

Harriet left Lilian with a neighbour while she and Alice attended the funeral. In addition to relatives, over a hundred miners had crowded into the tiny Hanham Baptist Church. Bill had been a well-liked man, kind, good-natured and caring for his fellow miners. The relatives sent wreaths of flowers, while the miners had collected and bought an Immortelle, a wreath of artificial flowers under a glass dome, which would be kept on Bill's grave at Hanham Baptist Burial Ground long after the flowers were dead.

A date was set for a Coroner's inquest, but had to be postponed, as the two eye-witnesses, Bill's brother George, and George Hooper's brother, Fredrick, were too ill to attend and give evidence. Both had suffered from the effects of the blast, and both had burns. The yellows and whites of early Spring gave way to the pinks and mauves of May, but this year it meant nothing to Harriet. Eventually the inquest took place a month after the event, on May 24th, and was meticulously reported in the Bristol Times and Record the following day. In addition to representatives of the mine's owners and the relatives of the deceased men were delegates from the Bristol Miners' Association and an H.M. Inspector of mines.

The inquest revealed that the four men had been working together, but only one of the four had a safety lamp; this had been left underground at the site where they were hewing when the men had come up for a break. The others were using candles, supplied by the company at the lamp-house that morning. The witnesses both stated they knew it was dangerous to use naked lights underground, although they knew of no rule which forbade their use. There had been no sign of gas when they first entered the mine that morning, they had seen the Examiner's mark at the site where they commenced working.

Both Fredrick Hooper and Bill's brother, George, described how they returned to the South Side after their break; neither heard the explosion, but suddenly found themselves knocked to the ground, and a great heat passed over their heads.

The Coroner then questioned Joseph Jones, the man who had examined the area for gas that morning. He told the Court that he had been a miner for forty years, and was certain that his eyesight was good enough to see a 'cap' of gas in a lamp. There was no gas that morning. He had never had his lamp put out by gas in the pit. No, he had never received formal training nor taken an examination for his post as examiner, neither could he tell the court the proportions of gas to atmosphere which made an explosive mixture.

Another examiner, Joseph White, stated that he found some gas at the site on the day of the accident, during a work-break, but it was 'only a capful' and he did not think it necessary to have safety lamps for those working there. He did not know the proportions of gas to atmosphere for an explosive mixture. Harriet, listening to the man's testimony, wept silently, thinking that if this man had reported gas at the site, Bill might still be alive.

The mine manager, Mr Herbert Monks, told the Court that they had been installing lamps throughout the pit, and the whole area where the accident had occurred was now using locked lamps; the men had to be trained to use these lamps. Too late, thought Harriet. In thirty-nine years of operations, the mine had never had such a tragic accident, he said. Complacent? Harriet wondered. Anyway, whatever they said, it would not bring Bill back again. She left the Court quietly and took her grief home.

Harriet had loved Bill with her entire being; she had lived for him. The rosy glow of first love and the fire of their passion had never worn away, for either of them. Her heart always quickened as he approached, her days were long when he was at work. Other women would rejoice to have the day to themselves, but never Harriet. Sundays and public holidays had been golden to her. Somehow she had always found enough money to buy a scrap of dress fabric at the market, to make a new blouse for each public holiday; that way she could always dress well and make him proud of her. 'Women who let themselves go only have themselves to blame when their husbands look elsewhere,' she would say, without compunction.

Suddenly the sun had gone out of her world. She was a widow of twenty-six, with two small children. She had a little money put aside, in a tin under the bed. Her father, George Bolt, had given her a small sum after the funeral 'to help tide you over'. The funeral expenses had been covered by the local miners' Friendly Society, to which Bill belonged, and a small insurance Harriet had taken out, of a half-pence a week. Her in-laws living next door would never see her starve but Harriet was too independent a spirit to rely on others. Besides which, she would not be able to pay the rent on her cottage for many more weeks.

She talked over her situation with her mother-in-law. There was no employment for women in the area, unless Harriet took domestic work, which she was reluctant to do. Mrs Fricker would have helped with the children, but she said that Bill's father was thinking of changing jobs and moving away. The death of his son had frightened and upset him more deeply than many realised; although he had so many children, he was a family man who cared for each one as an individual, and had seen Bill as most like himself. He was talking of moving to South Wales, said Mrs Fricker, where miners' wages were higher and their Union stronger, so possibly more attention would be paid to safety issues.

Harriet talked to representatives of the Miners Union. It was decided to make a claim for compensation from the pit owners, for Harriet and for Mrs Hooper. A few precedents had been set by now, so the representatives were hopeful that some money would be forthcoming. The weeks dragged by for Harriet; the bleakness of Bill's absence was exacerbated by the fractiousness of the children, who could not understand why their jolly, kind father no longer appeared. Alice was devastated by the loss of her father and did not speak for weeks. Harriet took her to the doctor in desperation, fearing that the tragedy had unbalanced the child in some way.

'It's a response young children sometimes make, Mrs Fricker, due to the shock,' he said. 'All you can do is to be as kind and loving as possible and try encourage her to go back to leading a normal life. Encourage her to play with other children—but don't be far away or she will fear that you have disappeared too. I realise that you have a huge burden to bear, but your little girl needs all the help you can give her at present. This problem will lift in a few weeks.'

Harriet dragged herself from chore to chore, feeling like an empty shell. Eventually her case was heard before a Tribunal, at which she was to appear. Apprehensive but determined, Harriet dressed with care that day; she had no wish to appear a wealthy widow, which she was not, but neither could she be seen as a drab, her pride would not let her. She stated her case clearly, that she was a young widow, with children of five and two years of age. Her savings were exhausted; she needed enough money for the three of them to live on. The Board, all men, conferred, and decided that Harriet did have a case, she should be awarded a lump sum, to be paid out to her at no more than five shillings a week. Harriet requested that the money should be awarded as a lump sum; she had in mind to open a grocer's shop, which would enable her to earn a living while caring for the children. The Board conferred again; they saw in Harriet a young, attractive, woman who might conceivably squander all the money and then become destitute, in spite of their generosity. No, the Board declined to pay a lump sum; the reason given was that as Harriet was young and therefore inexperienced with money, she might dispose of it too quickly and subsequently have to rely on charity, or go into the Poor House.

'Can't manage my money!' Harriet thought indignantly, but she was too dispirited to take issue with the Board. 'If I had been a man of twenty-six they wouldn't have said that. Why are we women so looked down on? We do as much if not more than men to hold family together.'

Far away in London, other women were fighting for voting rights for women, in an attempt to begin a process of equality, but Harriet knew little of this. Over the next few years it would seep into her consciousness, but she would still feel too disempowered to take positive action.

Harriet decided to move back to Bedminster; at least she would have her own family around her. Tearfully she said goodbye to her father- and mother-in-law, who were packing up to move to Crumlin, in South Wales, where Mr Fricker had found a house and a job at the local pit. Bill's brother George and his wife Saranne were planning to move back towards Bristol; he was enquiring about a job at the Whitehall Colliery.

Harriet's mother and father had offered her rooms in the family home in Whitehouse Lane, which Harriet viewed as a temporary measure. Her father was far too short-tempered to live happily with two young children in the house. Harriet's allowance from the Board would pay for their food and clothing for the children, but little else. She knew she would have to supplement her income, but how, with two small children, one of which was not yet school age?

Two little orphans
Alice, age about 5 years, and Lilian, age about 3 years

Chapter 4

A SECOND HAPPINESS

As GEORGE Bolt grew older, he gradually reduced his drinking—in fact, regretted that he had ever done so, especially since he had become a martyr to gout.

'Ah, Sarah,' he sometimes said wistfully, 'if only I hadn't been such a fool and wasted so much money, we could have been living in the lap of luxury now.' Sarah sniffed and thought, not luxury perhaps, but I wouldn't have had to work so hard in the past to keep the family together. Their two younger sons, William and Arthur, still lived at home. Harriet's sister, Alice, and her husband rented the house next door to George and Sarah Bolt; their first baby, a boy, was born the week before Harriet returned to Bedminster to live.

Sarah welcomed her daughter home, made a cup of tea, and gave Alice and Lilian a home-made cake each. Harriet looked around the home she had left six years ago, to enter married life with Bill. Little did she think she would ever return there to live. George was home from work with a bad dose of gout; he sat in the front parlour with his foot on a footstool. The sawmills had sent him some designs to work on at home; George had become an able draughtsman and nowadays spent more time at his desk than in the yard.

'Harriet, don't let the children get near my foot. Keep them in the other room.'

'All right, father.' Harriet shepherded the girls back to the kitchen.

'I expect you will go in and see Alice and the baby after you've had your tea,' Sarah said to Harriet; she was obviously worried about something. 'Have a look at the back of the baby's head, it's black. See what you think it is.'

'Black!' echoed Harriet. 'What do you mean, black skin?'

'Not exactly,' Sarah tried to explain. 'Sort of like blood under the skin, but it's black. I'm wondering if it's a fall she had while she was pregnant has caused it.'

'I didn't know she had a fall,' said Harriet.

'Well, not really a fall. You know how our Alice always used to rock her chair on the back legs when she finished her dinner? Your father was always telling her about it. She was doing it one day, and that fool Jim thought it would be funny to catch his foot under the chair and stop her.' Sarah had the same high opinion of Jim as Harriet. 'Anyway, he mistimed it and tipped her chair over backwards. She fell hard on her back, couldn't walk for a week. She was about six months at the time.'

'The fool!' Harriet put down her cup and went next door to see her sister.

Alice seemed well and was planning the baby's christening for the following week; he was to be named Edward Stanley. She and Jim were delighted to have a son.

'I think if it had been a daughter he would not have been so keen,' said Alice. 'But all men want sons, don't they?' Harriet averted her eyes. 'Has mother told you he has this black patch on his head?' She removed the baby's bonnet to show Harriet. It was as Sarah had described, a bluish black patch of rough skin. Harriet had never seen anything like it before.

'It doesn't seem to worry him,' said Alice. 'He sleeps well and feeds well.'

No more was said about the blemish, and plans continued for the christening. A gown was borrowed for the baby, and a bonnet. Alice dressed for Church, then dressed the baby in his borrowed finery. She laid him carefully on her double bed, while she fastened her new shoes. When she went to pick up her baby son, he was dead. She screamed at the top of her voice.

Jim, her mother and Harriet, who had all been waiting downstairs to go to the Church, rushed to her, but no one could revive the baby. Jim ran for the doctor, but the child was pronounced dead. The doctor suggested that the 'blemish' may well have been the external sign of something wrong with the brain, which had proved fatal.

Alice was distraught. She and Harriet cried together, for Alice's dead son and Harriet's dead husband. Nineteen-eleven was a bad year for them.

Harriet's eldest daughter was still not talking, four months after her father's death. Harriet took her to see the family doctor in Bedminster, a kindly man who had known her from childhood and sympathised with her current position. Lilian was also presenting problems, crying at the least little incident and seeming generally unhappy.

Dr Hill recognised that both children's problems stemmed from recent upsetting events; he reassured Harriet that Alice's speech would return to normal, but it might take several more months. Lilian was upset by all the changes, including the differences in her sister.

He spent more time talking to Harriet, trying to help her reconcile to Bill's death, and her new role as a combined mother/father figure. He saw Harriet as a strong young woman, who had been dealt a body-blow and needed a new goal for her regeneration.

'How about training as a midwife?' he suggested, knowing that Harriet was no stranger to birthing. 'We could do with some extra help in the Practice. Can you find someone to mind your children?'

'I could ask my mother,' Harriet replied thoughtfully The idea of a career appealed to her, especially as the hopes of owning her own shop had been dashed. She went home and asked her mother if she would look after the children, while she trained as a midwife.

'No, I'm sorry but I won't,' Sarah replied. 'I've had my children and brought them up; I've done with all that now. I don't really feel well enough to chase round after two small children, Harriet. Dr Hill says I have a weak heart, and my breathing is very bad some days. Besides, these are your children, you look after them. They need you, they've already lost a father.' So Harriet's ambitions for a career were quashed at conception, and she continued her frugal hand-to-mouth grey existence.

She began to wonder whether living at her parents' house was the best possible environment for her children. Her father had never been an easy man to live with, and expected everyone to accommodate his whims, to be quiet and polite at all times and still held to the Victorian maxim that 'children should be seen and not heard'. Alice and Lilian were not used to this; their father had encouraged them to be boisterous, to play naturally and noisily and to laugh out loud.

Harriet confided these fears to her brother, George Henry, on a visit to his home with the girls. They were playing happily with his son, Georgie-boy, who was two years older than Alice; as an only child he appreciated playmates. Teresa was in the kitchen, making tea.

'Why don't you come and live here?' he asked. 'Since Teresa's mother died last year we have a spare bedroom, big enough for you and the girls. Perhaps you could help Teresa with the housework, then we wouldn't need to charge you rent. It would be a help to us as well as a help to you.'

'Well, let's see what Teresa thinks,' Harriet replied cautiously, thinking that as Teresa was so undomesticated it would be she who was running the house, with possibly help from Teresa. But it was a kind offer, Harriet loved her brother and was very fond of Teresa, who could not help her dislike of housewifely duties.

Teresa was happy with the idea as she was fond of Harriet and her children. Georgie-boy had recently started school, so she would have company during the day, and welcomed help with running the house. 'It will be lovely to have you here, Harriet,' she said, 'when can you move in? Do you have any furniture you want to bring?'

The details were discussed and George Henry returned with Harriet to break the news to their mother.

'It's not that I don't want to live here, Ma,' she explained, 'but I feel it's such a difficult situation for father, having two young children around. I can't keep shushing them all the time, or Alice will never start to talk properly. And with William and Arthur at home you have more than enough to do here.'

Sarah was reluctant to see Harriet move, but saw the sense of the argument. When George returned from work that night she told him of the new arrangements.

'If that's what she wants, that's fine by me,' he said gruffly, privately thinking of the peaceful Sundays he could once again expect. 'Our George is a good son, to be looking after his sister like that.' The following week Harriet packed their clothes, William borrowed a horse and cart and they moved their few belongings to 107 Phillip Street.

At the time that Harriet returned to Bedminster to live, after her husband's death, her brother William was seventeen years old and worked as a fitter's apprentice at Wills tobacco factory; Arthur was eleven and still at school, where he was an able pupil. His teacher suggested he should stay at school an extra year, which would ensure him an office job. George and Sarah Bolt were proud of their clever son.

By the time William was eighteen he had matured into a personable, good-looking young man, and had no shortage of attractive young girls fluttering their eyelashes at him. One such young lady was Elvina Lewis, age eighteen, the youngest of a family of six children. Her parents owned two shops, one a fresh fish shop, the other a fried fish shop. Isaac Lewis, her father, was a lively, energetic man. As a young man he had been a stonemason, and had moved to Bristol from London to work on the restoration of St Mary Redcliffe Church and other building work in the area. He had met Alice Trim, married her and stayed in Bristol. Isaac had identified a gap in the Bristol market—there were no fried fish shops, which were becoming increasingly popular at the time he had left London. Alice's father was a butcher, he liked Isaac's energy and business acumen and helped him set up his first shop. This was such a success Isaac and Alice soon took over a second shop. Every morning except Sunday he went to the fish market at six o'clock, to make the best purchases of the day, taking them direct to the fresh fish shop at 93 Lawrence Hill, which was managed by George Fifoot. Here Isaac collected the unsold fish from the previous day and took them to his fried fish shop at 75 Lawrence Hill where he operated the fryers; his wife served the customers, but none of his six children worked in the shop.

Mrs Lewis was a short, plump woman, with tiny hands and feet. She wore numerous rings on her fingers, even when serving customers. Her bedecked fingers moved quickly and accurately over their purchases, ensuring that customers all obtained equal portions—in fact, some said they thought she counted the chips. Mrs Lewis was not going to give away their hard-earned profits; although money was not in short supply, there was always a float of £1,000 in cash under the bed, which was a huge sum of cash in 1911. She was careful with her husband's money, although she did have her little extravagances when it came to herself and her family. She liked jewellery and clothes, and when she went on a day's charabanc outing, she paid extra to have the coach pick her up at her front door, rather than walk to the meeting point. Her daughters always had fine clothes; the two elder girls, Maud and Mabel, always travelled to London to buy their handmade shoes. Maud had worked as a book-keeper before her marriage, but neither Mabel nor Elvina had considered looking for a job. Both of the older girls had made 'good' marriages, Mabel to a man who owned a butcher's shop and Maud to a factory manager. The two older Lewis sons, Uriah and Charles were both married and had children. Uriah, named after Alice's father, worked as a railway porter at Temple Meads Station and Charles was a butcher, currently negotiating to buy his own shop. The youngest son Frederick, a carpenter and cabinet-maker, was still unmarried and lived at home.

Fred was twenty-nine, an age by which a young man would be expected to be married; he had been engaged once, but had broken off the engagement. He had been sent to London by the firm of carpenters and joiners he worked for, and was only able to return home at weekends. One weekend he finished early and caught the train back to Bristol on Friday afternoon. He walked from Temple Meads direct to his fiancee's house, but she was not at home. On making enquiries, he found that she was out with another young man, and his informant said that this was not the first time. Fred did not wait to see her; he mounted the bicycle he had bought her a few weeks earlier, and rode home to Lawrence Hill. The engagement was over. Since then Fred had not looked for a serious relationship. He was a sociable young man, with many friends, keen on sports, especially fishing, and indoor pursuits, such as cards.

Elvina had mentioned to her parents that William Bolt had asked her to walk out with him. Mr and Mrs Lewis decided that it would be a good idea to meet the young man and invited him to tea one Sunday. William asked whether he might bring his sister, Harriet; maybe he needed moral support, or felt it would show serious intent on his part and the involvement of his family.

William was obviously given approval during Sunday tea, as Mr and Mrs Lewis permitted the two young people to go for a Sunday stroll together. As Harriet donned her coat to go home, Fred offered to walk home with her.

'Oh no, there's no need,' she said. 'It's not far to go, and it's still light.' But Fred insisted. As they walked to Bedminster, Harriet talked to Fred about the circumstances of her widowhood, and her two children. She found him kind and easy to talk to. When she paused outside her brother's house, where she had left the two girls with Teresa, Fred asked if he might see her again.

'I don't think so,' Harriet said doubtfully. 'After all, I have my two little girls to look after.'

'Bring them too,' said Fred. 'How about next weekend? It's a

Bank Holiday, we could all go to the zoo.'

The Bank Holiday was fine and bright. Fred called to collect Harriet and the girls, and they boarded the tram for Bristol Zoo. Alice, who was six, was very excited; she loved animals and dragged her mother from cage to cage to see the exhibits. Lilian, who was only three, was tired by the time they reached the zoo. She seemed more scared than enchanted by the animals in the cages. She started to whine, and would not even be placated by the promise of the picnic lunch Harriet had packed. Fred hoisted her onto his shoulders and carried her around for the rest of the day. He was not a big man, only five feet seven inches tall, and slightly built, with fair hair and blue eyes. Harriet looked at him out of the corner of her eye; Lilian was still snivelling. 'He won't want to see us again,' she thought, but she was wrong. In the subsequent weeks, Fred was a frequent caller; he brought presents for the girls, and took Harriet out whenever she could spare the time.

Harriet went to see her sister, Alice, who had just been safely delivered of a little girl whom she planned to call Rose.

'She's a beautiful baby, Alice, and she looks so healthy,' said Harriet, kissing the baby's fingers.

'She is lovely, and so good,' agreed Alice. 'Please God she'll stay that way. Now tell me about you and Fred—is it serious?'

'Well possibly; he seems very fond of me and of the children too. But there's nothing more to say yet, and it's early days for me, it's only eighteen months since Bill died.'

'Well yes,' said Alice sagely, 'but you are still young and you and your girls have your whole lives ahead of you.'

Although Harriet encouraged Alice and Lilian to accept Fred, she ensured that they never forgot their real father. His photograph was prominently displayed in their home and she regularly took them to visit his grave, to tidy it and put fresh flowers. Fred showed no jealousy of the affection with which she spoke of her first husband. One day Harriet returned from a visit to Bill's grave, visibly upset. She told Fred that the grave was covered in refuse which had been thrown over the wall which divided the cemetery from the lane to the Chapel. Worse still, the Immortelle on the grave had been broken; it was the only indication of Bill's name, as Harriet had never been able to afford a headstone. Fred decided the problem had arisen because the grave was undefined; he made a hardwood frame for the grave and installed it. He and Harriet then weeded and tidied the grave and planted a small shrub. Harriet decided he was the kindest man she knew, her love for him was growing steadily.

In August 1913 they were married, Harriet wore a brown silk-taffeta dress which would be suitable for 'best' afterwards. William and Elvina, the progenitors of the romance, had parted company by this time, and Elvina had found a new beau. Elvina was thrilled at being instrumental in the match and insisted on being a witness at the wedding as there were to be no bridesmaids.

Harriet had loved her first husband, Bill, with the intensity and passion of her youth, a fierce love never known to some people. The flame of that passion was quenched by his death; in others it burns itself out or is transformed to a quiet affection, which simmers to old age, when those couples smile to each other, recalling the passion of their youth. Harriet loved Fred in a quiet, affectionate way—he was a quiet, affectionate man, so it suited him. The burning love she had known for Bill could never be recreated, it was a gift given only once.

Fred and Harriet planned to start married life in rented rooms but Fred's sister, Mabel, told them that there was a house to let next door to her and her husband, in Bloy Street, Easton. Fred and Harriet went to see it. There was a front parlour, dining room and tiny kitchen downstairs, and two bedrooms upstairs. At the back of the house there was an ample garden, outside toilet and a coalhouse.

'We could dig up the bottom part of this garden to grow our

own vegetables,' said Fred, 'have some flowers near the house.'

'That would be nice. These houses are smaller than the Victorian houses in Bedminster, and the ceilings are much lower,' observed Harriet.

'Yes, but the rent is cheap, if you can get used to the size of the rooms,' Fred replied.

As they did not have a great deal of furniture to accommodate, the room size was not really an issue and the family moved in a few weeks later. Bloy Street seemed much brighter an area than Bedminster, possibly due to the absence of tall, industrial buildings and factory chimneys. At that time there was little commerce or industry in the area, but Fred was able to ride his bicycle or take the tram to Murray's, near Old Market, where he worked. There was a school nearby, where Alice commenced, the Easton Board School; Harriet put Lilian's name down for the following year. The neighbours were friendly; Harriet joined the Mothers' Union with Fred's other married sister, Maud, who had two children at that time.

Harriet was also friendly with Mabel but was not keen on Mabel's husband, Richard. He was constantly trying to find fault with his wife, one of the issues being that she had produced no children; Mabel confided to Harriet that she too was concerned that they had been married a number of years and were still childless.

'Why don't you go and see a specialist?' Harriet asked her. There may be just a small thing wrong they could put right. I'm sure Richard would pay for that.'

Eventually Mabel consulted a specialist who told her that he could find nothing wrong with her.

'Send your husband to me,' he said, 'I think that may be where the fault lies.' Her husband, however, refused to go, but no longer rebuked Mabel about her childlessness.

Harriet became friendly with the elderly couple who ran the corner shop in Bloy Street. They were impressed by her careful housekeeping, she never owed money. She had told them about her parents' shop and they compared retail strategies. When the couple decided to retire, the following year, they asked Harriet if she would like to buy their shop, as they wanted her to have it.

Harriet discussed the idea with Fred; the shop had living accommodation, so they would not be paying rent, and food would be wholesale price, not retail. Fred's wages were enough for them to live on; Harriet would run the shop alone while the two girls were at school. Any surplus money they made in the shop would go towards paying off their loan. Harriet was a good manager and she had always wanted to own her own shop; they decided to ask Fred's parents if they would lend them the money, and Harriet went to see Fred's mother one morning.

'What!' cried Mrs Lewis. 'That would be throwing good money after bad! Three people have gone out of that shop bankrupt. No, I won't lend you money for that!'

'Well, I won't go bankrupt,' Harriet retorted, and marched out of the house, furious, knowing that there was enough money under the Lewis's bed to have bought two or three shops such as the one in Bloy Street. She went to see her mother next.

'If I had it, I would lend it to you,' said Sarah, 'and I know someone who will.' She took Harriet to see a friend of hers, Mrs Lavelle, who lent money from time to time. Harriet wondered whether she had provided a loan for their Bedminster shop, as she had been too young to be included in the full knowledge of the family finances at that time. Harriet's loan was soon arranged, and the repayments settled, at a very low rate of interest, as Mrs Lavelle knew and trusted Sarah and her daughter. The shop was purchased and the family moved across the road.

The shop area was large, being a corner building. At the back was a kitchen large enough for family meals. Upstairs was a parlour, and two large bedrooms. Behind the shop was a small concrete yard and the outside toilet; Fred would have to forgo his recent hobby of growing vegetables in the back garden. Harriet and Fred took the front bedroom, overlooking the street, while the girls shared the bedroom which overlooked the yard. Fred, being a cabinet-maker, made any extra furniture and shop fittings Harriet felt they needed.

Fred helped with the heavy work of the shop, lifting sacks of potatoes, flour and sugar, for all goods were supplied loose, and were weighed and packed in the shop. Harriet had always been quick at calculating money, since her childhood days of shopping for her mother, so weights and prices held no terrors for her. Having helped in her mother's shop, she was adept at patting butter with the wooden paddles and estimating how much cheese to cut with the wire, for each customer's requirements. The shop sold mainly groceries, and some greengroceries; dried peas were set to soak in a barrel, for sale by volume. She expanded the business into other areas not touched by the previous owners, they churned their own ice-cream (this became young Alice's job, as she liked to sample the outcome) and made toffee apples, which became well-known in the area.

The shop began to thrive. Harriet kept a careful eye on her customers, wherever possible not allowing them to run larger credit bills than they could afford. Many women would buy goods 'on tick' throughout the week, paying off their bills at the weekend, when their husbands received their wages. Harriet would not allow credit the following week unless the bill was paid. However, she was also kind, she would wrap and give away the ends of hams and other small items to families who needed help, perhaps the breadwinner was ill, or out-of-work. There were still customers who suddenly found they could not pay their bills, or needed to barter in exchange for food. In those cases, Harriet accepted goods in lieu of cash, frequently items such as ornaments, which she neither needed nor liked, but she realised the face-saving necessity of customers who could not take charity from those like herself, who could not really afford to give.

'The shop is providing a reasonable income,' said Fred, looking up from the books one Saturday evening. 'I do wonder whether I should give up work to help run the shop with you, dear.' He enjoyed his work as a carpenter, but most of his precious day off was spent in duties around the shop.

'I think we should be a little careful as yet,' Harriet urged. 'These are early days in the business; my father always worked at his job, while my mother looked after the shop.'

Of course, the difference there lay in the fact that George Henry had also worked in the shop and did the heavy work, but Fred was too mild-mannered a man to point out this difference. Instead he found his own solution.

Fred reappeared home from work at lunchtimes, from time to time. Murray's were on short time, he said, there wasn't enough work for all the men to be there full-time. On weekdays the shop was not overly busy, so he took his fishing tackle and went fishing. He usually caught enough fish for his tea, but Harriet would eat none of them, saying she didn't like 'river fish'. What she meant was she did not like the polluted rivers around Bristol where the fish swam.

Each Wednesday afternoon Harriet closed the shop and usually visited her mother or Alice, but one afternoon she went to the draper's, to buy dress fabric for the girls. She made all the girls' clothes and most of her own, which ensured that the family all looked tidy, if not affluent. She also 'laid aside' goods which she wanted at the drapers, bedlinen, tablecloths and the like, and paid a small sum each week; when the goods were paid up, she took them home. The draper's shop was in Old Market Street, where Harriet bumped into Mr Murray, Fred's employer.

'Hello, Mrs Lewis,' he said, raising his hat. ' How's Fred? I'm sorry he has been so poorly lately. We do miss him at work, you know, especially as we're so busy at present. Do ask him if he can get in soon.'

Harriet's mouth had dropped open, but she regained her composure enough to reply, 'Don't worry Mr Murray, he will be back at work tomorrow.'

And he was.

Harriet sensed that Fred's mother did not like her, and after the refusal to lend the money for the shop purchase, the feeling was reciprocated. However, Harriet always encouraged Fred to visit his mother regularly and to take Alice and Lilian with him on Sunday mornings, while she looked after the shop. Mrs Lewis had not wanted Fred to marry a widow with two children, but she had to admit, the girls were always polite and pleasant. She was pleased that they always called her 'grandma', and she gave them a penny each, every Sunday.

One Sunday morning Fred was not well enough to undertake his regular visit to his mother, as he had a cold and the wind was sharp. Harriet dressed the girls in their new fur-trimmed coats and sent them off to see their grandma, to explain that 'Daddy is poorly, and mummy is looking after the shop.'

'Be very careful crossing the main road,' Harriet admonished eight-year-old Alice. 'Don't let go of Lilian's hand. Come straight home, and be back by dinnertime. Don't talk to any strangers.'

'I know that, Ma. We never talk to strangers,' Alice replied, and set off, full of her own self-importance.

Sunday dinner was at mid-day, when Harriet shut the shop. Fred was still in bed, with his cold and a hot drink when the girls returned, in good time for their meal.

'Did your grandma like your new coats?' Harriet asked, as she removed the girls' coats and hung them on pegs.

'I think so,' said Alice. 'She said to us, "Is that what your mother spends my son's money on?" so I suppose she liked them.'

'What!' exclaimed Harriet. She repeated the story to Fred, as she shut the shop, and put on her outdoor shoes, coat and hat. 'I'm off to set your mother right. You and the girls have your dinners, don't wait for me.'

'Now don't go saying anything. It doesn't matter what she thinks. Don't make trouble in the family,' Fred urged.

'Me make trouble?' called Harriet as she shut the front door behind her.

Mrs Lewis was surprised to see Harriet, but before she could say anything, Harriet said: 'I thought you should know, Mrs

Lewis, that my daughters' clothes—including their new coats—are bought from the money I was awarded after their father's death down the mine. He died providing for them, Mrs Lewis. Your son merely has the pleasure of their company - free.'

Harriet flounced out of the Lewis's home and ensured that she saw her mother-in-law less often than before. She still encouraged Fred and the children to visit, as spite was not in Harriet's nature.

Chapter 5

THE WAR TO END ALL WARS

PATRIOTIC FEVER gripped the country, when war was declared in 1914. Over a million men enlisted between August and December, they said. Some of the Regulars had been sent to France within weeks of the declaration of war, others were being recalled from postings abroad, while the volunteers, Kitchener's New Army, were being trained. While many men had queued to enlist, to 'do their bit' for King and country, those who had good jobs held back. After all, it would all be over by Christmas; it would be easy to spare four months to serve the country in a just cause but what then? Few employers, especially in the smaller businesses, were promising to hold jobs open for men who enlisted, so would a man find himself out of work in a few months time?

1915

The Bolts were as patriotic as the next family but not eager for war. George Bolt, at nearly fifty-six, was too old to be expected to enlist, but George Henry and William both held jobs they did not wish to lose—William especially wanted to complete his apprenticeship - and Arthur was too young to sign up. Alice's husband, Jim, was keen to enlist in the Navy but Alice was expecting another baby. Little Violet was born in November 1914 and Jim susequently enlisted. Fred hesitated until 1915, feeling that his first duty was to Harriet and the children, but when the war was not over by Christmas and Murray's, his workplace, posted notices promising that jobs would be held open for all men enlisting, Fred broached the matter to Harriet.

She was visibly disturbed; having lost one husband to a violent death, she wanted Fred to take no risks. However, duty won, and Fred enlisted in the RASC in March, 1915. He was sent to Aldershot for training and sent Harriet a number of postcards: cartoon soldiers, scenes of the barracks and an airship.

'I am saving all the postcards you send me, in an album,' Harriet wrote to Fred. 'Please send as many as you can, especially if you are sent overseas.' This was the commencement of a new hobby for Harriet and her daughters, a fashionable hobby at the time.

Mid-August he was given home-leave, until embarcation at Avonmouth Docks, Bristol, for Southampton, and then onward to France. This only represented five months training, whereas Kitchener had said that his New Army should have ten months before reaching active service, but a number of battalions of the New Army were embarking at that time, and Fred went with them.

Fred's training at Aldershot mapped his wartime experiences. As an Army driver, he ferried provisions and men to the front, ran errands and occasionally took wounded men back from the front. He was also involved in mass troop transport from one position to the other or at times in organised retreats. For such a small, slightly-built man, Fred handled the heavy troop lorries well, wresting the heavy steering round muddy bends and through narrow channels. In convoy, he reasoned, best not to go first, in case of land mines. Too far back and you were likely to be the target of ground or air fire, as they had your position by then.

These new divisions were ordered to the Western Front, arriving in time for the battle at Loos, where sixty thousand British troops were killed or injured, due to inexperience and poor leadership. This prompted the reorganisation of divisions to include both Regular and New Army battalions. Although he was a member of the Service Corps, Fred was often working in the trenches.

He was grateful to have survived his first major battle, having lost several mates during the three weeks of that conflict. He knew he would be unable to write and describe the conditions there to Harriet, the mud to their knees, the stench, the ineffectual attacks, going forward and retreating; his letters would be censored. In addition, he did not want to alarm and upset her, so sent mainly postcards, trying to keep his communications light. Having entered the war with a will, Fred soon became as disenchanted and dispirited as other men who had been at the Front longer.

The men in the trenches knew that the Germans had used gas on the British troops at Ypres, and a primitive type of gas mask had been issued subsequently. Chlorine gas had been used at that time, which issued from the containers as a yellowish cloud. No one seemed to know what sort of gas might be used in future or what the effects would be. The British had used gas at Loos, in retaliation for Ypres, and gas was used sporadically by both sides subsequently, and largely ineffectually, as the follow-ups were badly executed; no one wanted to jump into enemy trenches which they had just filled with gas.

Fred's division, the 23rd, was involved in a minor skirmish towards the end of 1915. A conventional battle had commenced, when shells landing in the British trenches exuded gas. The cry went up, 'Gas, gas,' and men scrambled to don their gas masks. Some ran back from the frontline trenches, rubbing their streaming eyes, in fact rubbing the gas into their eyes. Fred was in the second line of trenches, and was also affected before he could put on his mask, but was fortunate enough not to have permanent repercussions from the gas attack. This attack was more tentative and had far less devastating effects than those at Ypres, as the men were better prepared this time. Treatment was given at the Field Hospital, then Fred applied for home leave for rest and recuperation over Christmas, 1915.

Harriet and the children were delighted to see him; it was an unexpected Christmas present for them. Fred seemed very quiet, not wanting to talk much about the war. He did tell Harriet and

Frederick Lewis, during The Great War

his parents that conditions in the trenches were bad, and casualties were far higher than the British press had been disclosing. Although he seemed unaffected by the gas, he had a tiresome cough. Harriet was unsure whether to attribute this to the gas or the increased number of Woodbines he was smoking. These were issued to the troops, Fred told her, so everyone smoked constantly.

'But you never light more than two men's cigarettes with one match,' he told Harriet. 'By the third cigarette, the Germans have fixed your position and a sniper will get you.'

Fred, Harriet and the children went to the family Christmas party at George Henry's house. All three of Harriet's brothers had numerous questions for Fred, as conscription was to be introduced in 1916; both George Henry and William had decided to enlist, as their employers were promising to hold jobs open for them, for after the war. Fred tried to neither encourage nor discourage them from joining up; he had seen so many men killed he did not want to feel responsible for encouraging them into life-threatening situations. He tried to answer their questions honestly, without over-dramatisation, as this was Fred's way. William, as an unmarried twenty-two year old, would be liable for the first draft; George Henry, as a married man, would be called up in May.

Harriet's youngest brother, Arthur, who was only seventeen, was telling Fred his plans to join up within the year, as soon as they would take him. Harriet listened silently, watching her mother's lined face, and hoping that Arthur's girlfriend, Elsie Vickers, would persuade him to stay at home.

The gloom of the war was obliterated as the party progressed. George Henry had obtained a keg of beer from his employers, Georges' Brewery, as his Christmas gift; his son Georgie-boy, although only eleven years old, kept them all entertained with piano renditions of popular tunes which he played by ear, having inherited the Bolts' musical talents. Harriet chatted to her sister, Alice, and George Henry's wife, Teresa. Alice's two daughters,

Rose who was three years old and Violet just over a year, played happily with Harriet's girls. Harriet noticed her father was not drinking very much, perhaps his gout was troubling him again; still, George Henry seemed to have taken up his father's mantle and was downing pint after pint, but he grew more jovial with each drink rather than aggressive.

Alice's husband, Jim, now serving on HMS Mons, had been unable to come home over Christmas. Alice was resigned to being alone as her parents lived next door, and as she confided to Harriet, 'Jim's no help with the children, anyway, when he is home. Perhaps it might have been different if our son had lived.' Harriet doubted it.

Fred, Harriet and the children visited his parents on Boxing Day, to reassure them he was fit and well. Bridges had been mended between Harriet and her mother-in-law while Fred had been away; she visited them every few weeks to ensure they had heard from him, and to pass on any news she had. Fred's elder brother, Uriah, was reconciled to being conscripted when they called married men; his work on the railways might have given him exemption, but he decided he should 'do his bit'. Charles, his other brother, had also resigned himself to conscription. He had so little to sell in his butcher's shop, he told Fred, he might as well close it down for the duration of the war.

The day after Boxing Day was Lilian's sixth birthday. Harriet made a sponge cake and iced it, and they played games with the two girls.

1916

By January 17th 1916, Fred returned to Folkestone, ready to embark for France. The next day he sent Harriet a postcard from Folkestone, to say that he had to stay there overnight, as there were too many soldiers for the boat. The following day he sailed for France and rejoined his division in the trenches on the Western Front, in France.

Nineteen-sixteen dragged on, a continuum of constant bombardments, noise, mud and poor food. The recruitment drive was stepped up at home; more employers promised to hold open jobs for men who enlisted. William enlisted in the Wiltshire Regiment, 1st Battalion, and after his initial training was sent to the Western Front near Arras, where the Regiment had suffered casualties during the May conflicts there. The division proceeded towards the Bapaume area of France in 1917, where it remained for the duration of the war. George Henry, in spite of having a wife and young son, also felt that he should come forward, joined the Ordinance Corps, and began his training.

Whenever circumstances were favourable, many regiments operated a system of keeping men at the Front for four or five days, then sending them back to billets for the equivalent number of days for respite. When the men were billeted in villages behind the front line, Fred realised that the villages still had food to sell. This was useful information, he thought, there *was* food available in France, maybe not plentiful, but imaginatively and lovingly prepared and cooked. It could be purchased, given the right approach.

Consequently, Fred and his friends went in search of food as diligently as many others looked for sex. The French housewives were ingenious in the use of ingredients in their cooking. Most of the sheep, cows and goats had been appropriated long ago by the army, French, Allied or German, but there were still wild rabbits and hares for trapping, and almost certainly other mammals which were never named found their way into the pot. Old boiling fowls, past laying, were simmered long and slow, with a helping of wine. Snails were washed, boiled and dressed with garlic. Rice pudding was cooked until solid, left until cold, then turned out on a plate and cut like cake. Fred developed a liking for these continental dishes, to the extent that he enquired about how to prepare and cook the dishes, which greatly amused the French housewives.

He found that his funds were dwindling, as he paid for extra food. Some of his wages were sent directly to Harriet, he only collected 'spending money'. He wrote to Harriet, telling her he found the army food unpalatable, and asking her to send him extra money for food, if she could mange it. After all, he reasoned, she also had money coming in from the shop, so there should be some to spare. What he did not realise, as few men at the Front knew, was that times were hard at home; frequently the shop had to be shut because Harriet had nothing to sell.

The story of Britain in the First World War has been told many times: how the mood of the country changed from the initial enthusiasm for enlistment, encouraged by young women giving out white feathers to men not in uniform, to one of fear and anger when news revealed so many were killed in the first year or so. The mood of optimism in the country had to be rekindled by changes in top military personnel, recruitment drives and, finally, conscription; however the increase in enlistments was only matched by more deaths or injuries. New to the home country was the sight of men returning with shell-shock, a sight never seen in previous wars. These mentally scarred men were sent for rest and recuperation, often for insufficient lengths of time, before they were returned to the front, sometimes being given the choice of return to the front or imprisonment, with its accompanying dishonour. Men who lost their nerve under fire and ran from the Front were captured and shot by their compatriots as deserters.

News of victories was enhanced, while news of defeats and retreats was scarce, as the Government sought to imply that Britain, with God and right on her side, was bound to win. Pictures and news of heroic deeds were featured, while the truths about mud, privations and deaths were seldom told.

As more and more men were sent to the front, jobs were taken up by women. Work in the munitions factories, heavy work in industry and agriculture, which they would not have contemplated prior to 1914; the face of the women's world was changing, although they did not yet have the vote. Harriet still ran the shop, throughout the War. Times became harder, as more food was sent to the Front, and there were fewer people at home producing it. When she received Fred's letter, requesting money for food, she frowned. George Henry seemed to be managing well on his Army pay. His wife, Teresa, received her allowance, and George sometimes sent home extra money 'for my beautiful wife and my darling little Georgie-boy'. Harriet sniffed. While George Henry was away, Teresa saw no point in housework and spent most of her time sitting and eating. Consequently she had put on a great deal of weight, and the beauty of her youth was being obliterated.

Harriet sighed and re-read Fred's letter. Of course she knew that her brother was a gambler; he ran a Crown and Anchor board during the War, which ensured that, like a bookmaker, he was always on the winning side. Fred, she knew, would have a little bet on a game of cards, but rarely lost money as he was a skilful player. She considered carefully and decided that her husband must really need the money for food. For that purpose she sympathised; one of her favourite sayings was 'you can always promise the back, but you can't promise the belly' meaning that you could do without new clothes but not food.

How to economise was the question. She still had a little of the money left from the settlement on the death of her first husband, so that would pay for clothes for the girls. With no social life of her own, she needed few new clothes herself and was adept at making-do; if she needed a new blouse she could make one from a couple of yards of fabric from the draper's. Food would come from the shop, at cost price, but loan repayments for the shop still had to be met. Harriet worked out her costs carefully, trying to minimise the problems at home. 'After all,' she reasoned, 'those poor devils at the front have enough problems without knowing ours.' With her usual resourcefulness, Harriet tightened belts at home, and sent Fred money for food. Maybe it was the blessing of a full belly which helped Fred resist most of the common illnesses of soldiers in the trenches and helped him survive those which he contracted.

Fred's division, meanwhile, was preparing for the nightmare of mud and death which became known as the Battle of the Somme, which raged from July 1st to November 18th, where they went into action no less than five times. After the first day of battle, British casualties numbered 58,000, but by July 11th they had secured the first line of German trenches. Fred never understood how he managed to survive when so many around him were killed or injured. He was ordered to drive an ambulance of wounded men to Boulogne, for transfer to England for hospitalisation there. On reaching Boulogne he was instructed to accompany the casualties to England, where he could stay overnight and return to France the next day. He sent Harriet a postcard, in an envelope, so that he could leave the place-name, Verdun, visible. 'I am in London overnight,' he wrote, 'will explain later. Having a good feed.' The next day he returned to France, back to the Somme, where the autumn brought rain and murderous mud.

Arthur Stanley Bolt, photo taken before going to the Front in The Great War. Killed in action.

George Henry Bolt, during The Great War

1917

Harriet had always maintained her friendship with Ellen, although the two women met rarely, as Harriet was busy in the shop and Ellen worked as a cook-housekeeper six and a half days a week. During the early part of the war, Ellen began 'walking out' with a young man who worked at the Bristol docks; as this was considered an essential job, he was not expected to enlist. However, by 1917 the call for more manpower in the Army meant that Alfred received his call-up papers. Hastily, the two were married before he was sent to France, and rented a small cottage in Hereford Street, Bedminster.

Young Arthur had married his young lady, Elsie, at the end of 1916, shortly before his eighteenth birthday, and moved in with her and her mother in York Road. A few weeks later he had enlisted with the Machine Gun Brigade and had been sent to the Western Front the following May. Unknown to his family at home, his division was preparing for the third battle of Ypres, where bombardment was planned for the beginning of August, but was brought forward to the commencement of July.

Fred's Division moved north in 1917, towards Ypres, and the usual four days on, four days off resumed, away from the heat of constant battle. It was during one of his respites at Watten, behind the Ypres lines, that Fred met Adrienne, a plump, motherly woman some ten years older than himself, whose husband had been killed during the early months of the war. She invited Fred for a meal with her and her daughter, a young woman in her late teens. She was an excellent cook, and Fred was grateful for a change from army food. The two managed to communicate, with the smattering of French Fred had acquired, and Adrienne's few words of English. She offered to cook other meals for Fred, which he insisted on paying for. Fred learned from Adrienne how to cook many of the French dishes, and discovered a liking for rare meat. Adrienne, in return, lavished affection on Fred, regarding him as a substitute companion for her absent husband. They shared companionship, but never a bed, as Fred felt he could not be unfaithful to Harriet. They showed each other family photographs, and Adrienne cooed over the pictures of Alice and Lilian. Fred never told Adrienne they were not his daughters, as he always regarded them as such, but in his heart he thought: if I die in this war, there is nothing left of me, it is as though I had never been. Perhaps if I ever get home, Harriet and I could have a child together.

In addition to the hazards of warfare, life in the trenches threatened the men with numerous diseases. In June 1917 Fred began to feel ill, and had a strangely sore throat. He collapsed one morning and his friends carried him to the First Aid post. The medical officer had seen other men with the same symptoms and immediately diagnosed diphtheria. Fred was initially taken to an isolation ward attached to the field hospital, but was then transported to a specialist hospital south of the Front.

For several weeks Harriet heard nothing from Fred; she was worried, as he was a man who wrote home at least once a week. Both he and Harriet blessed their early schooling, that they could both read and write. 'You would be surprised,' Fred had told her, 'how many men here cannot read. I am often asked to read letters from home to them, and to write their replies.' The absence of letters and postcards worried Harriet and she began to wonder if he had been killed. Eventually Fred's commanding officer wrote to Harriet, to tell her that he was in hospital with diphtheria. She took the letter to show her mother, who looked at her gravely.

'My dear,' she said to Harriet, 'I think you have to realise that this is a very serious illness. Not many people recover from it; you may lose your husband.' Harriet had thought as much; Sarah's words released the floodgates and she cried copiously. When she felt strong enough she took the letter to show Fred's parents; she did not add Sarah's comments, but left them to draw their own conclusions. She told her children that 'Daddy is ill, but they have taken him to a hospital to try to make him better.'

Fred was so ill that he had little recollection of his early days in hospital. Gradually he began to recover, although many of the other diphtheria sufferers were not so fortunate. The illness left him very weak, and he stayed at the hospital for some time until he was allowed home leave to recuperate for two weeks.

Harriet usually visited her parents weekly, and knew how anxious they were about their sons in the Army. Harriet was worried about her mother; she had had a weak heart for years, the strain of all this must be taking its toll. Her father, too, was beginning to look haggard. Alice had confided to Harriet that their father called at her house every day on his way home from work, to ask if there had been any news from the Front, always expecting the worst.

'This uncertainty will kill your mother,' he said, shaking his head, but his own anxieties were obvious, as he threw his lunch sandwiches into Alice's bin before going home. 'I can't eat midday,' he said. 'Don't tell your mother.'

Harriet and Fred went to see them so they could have first hand information on life in the trenches. Fred tried to minimise the discomforts, so as not to upset the older couple. After all, he reasoned, what could they do? They would only worry; Harriet had told him they were both constantly anxious, but not discussing their worries together, on the assumption it would only upset the other.

Sarah told Fred she had sent a food parcel to William for Christmas, which included a large Christmas pudding, to share with his friends.

'Food parcels are always very welcome at the Front,' Fred told her, and reassured her these were always delivered to the correct person. 'The Field Post Offices are highly efficient; letters and parcels are delivered promptly.' He did not tell Sarah that the pudding would probably have to be eaten cold, sitting in the trenches, as there were few facilities for heating food efficiently.

'Socks are always useful, too,' he added, 'we never seem to have enough socks.' He did not add that the constant water in the trenches meant constantly wet socks, which rotted away, causing 'trench foot' and other ills.

Fred and Harriet visited Teresa, George Henry's wife, who told them he had been sent to India. Harriet was mystified by this information.

'Surely it is Europe, not India, that's under attack. Why India?'

'Ah well,' Fred explained, 'current thinking suggests that India might be invaded from the north, through the Khyber Pass, and the Jewel would be lost from the Empire's crown. We don't want to lose India while we are busy helping Europe. When the Regulars were withdrawn from India to send to the Western Front, they had to send replacement troops from the Territorials and volunteers to replace them. They are stationed there to ensure this there's no invasion from the north, and also to prevent any uprising against British rule, as there has been trouble like that in the past'.

'And have there been any problems?' asked Teresa.

'Not to my knowledge,' Fred replied. 'In fact, the Indian troops are coming to join us in Europe, all credit to them too, they must find it very cold and wet compared to their country. Some of them wear turbans in the trenches, instead of tin hats, because of their religion; they must be very brave, a turban's no protection against bullets.'

Harriet looked at Fred, wonderingly. He was abroad, in a foreign country where the local people spoke a language he did not comprehend, he was meeting all sorts of other people from civilisations unknown to Harriet, and he did not seem fazed by it, neither was he criticizing their differences. Harriet was sure she could not have been so open-minded. She remembered her father telling her that his grandfather had run to Bristol docks, as a boy, to see the French prisoners brought to Bristol by ship during the Napoleonic wars, because rumour had it that the Frenchmen had tails. How perceptions of foreigners had changed in the last hundred years, Harriet thought. And politics, we are now fighting to relieve that very country from German occupation.

The Wednesday before Fred was due to return to the Front they closed the shop at lunchtime, and went for a stroll together in Eastville Park, where much of the grassland had been ploughed to grow vegetables. Neither talked much, as both knew their separation was imminent. Harriet took Fred's arm for comfort, and gave it a little squeeze, he smiled at her in return, then looked around him at the parkland, taking in the scent of the new-mown grass and the lime trees. His mind instantly contrasted it with the sights and sounds he would soon return to, the mud in the trenches, the constant sounds of gunfire, the stench and the sight of broken and bleeding bodies. He shook his head; it was another world and he wouldn't think about it yet.

Fred returned to his Division, which had been engaged in the early stages of the Third battle of Ypres; in fact he was only a few miles away from Arthur, although neither knew of the proximity of the other. After two further weeks at the Front, Fred's Division was relieved and prepared to embark for Italy. Arthur, meanwhile, moved forward with the 248th Company, setting up machine gun placements. On the 20th September, after Fred had left for Italy, Arthur and his unit engaged in the battle of Menin Road Ridge, as it later became known. A precise aim at the machine gun placement blew Arthur to pieces. His mate recognised Arthur's wedding ring on his hand, removed it and sent it with a letter to Elsie, telling her how bravely her husband had died. Elsie and the Bolt family were devastated. Arthur was the youngest son, and had been at the Front only a few months; now he was gone. Fred had been so ill; they had thought he was dying or dead. Anxiety levels were now raised about William and George Henry, and Alice's husband, Jim. Sarah Bolt was inconsolable over the death of her youngest son.

Harriet wrote to Fred to tell him of Arthur's death, hoping he would not take it too badly. But Fate had not finished with the Bolts in 1917. Harriet woke early one morning, a few days after the news of Arthur's death, to the rattle of small stones being thrown at her bedroom window. She opened the window and looked out to see her sister, Alice, clutching her coat around her.

'Whatever is it, Alice?' she asked.

'It's father, he's very ill,' Alice replied. 'Come quick, Harriet.'

'Father? Surely you mean mother! Wait a minute, I'll come down.'

Harriet hurried downstairs and opened the door to her sister, who told her that her mother had called her in the early hours of the morning, from their house next door, to say that their father had been taken ill. Alice had run for the doctor, and then run on to call Harriet.

'What? You've run all the way here from Whitehouse Lane!' exclaimed Harriet. 'Here, sit down while I get dressed, I'll come straight away. The early trams will be running in a few minutes, we'll ride back. Who is with your children?'

'I expect they're still asleep—anyway, Jim is home on five days leave; he arrived yesterday,' said Alice. 'He'll cope, till I get back.'

Harriet woke her daughters and told them she was going to their grandfather, who was ill. 'You need not go to school today. Stay indoors till I get back; don't open the shop for anyone.' Harriet posted a note on the shop door 'Closed due to illness'.

By the time the two women arrived at their parents' house, George Bolt was dead. The doctor was there and told them he had suffered a stroke. Sarah was almost hysterical; the doctor gave her a draft to calm her, and Alice took her next door and put her to bed.

When George Bolt was buried, Sarah moved in to live with Alice; her house and most of her furniture was sold. She seemed like a broken woman. Harriet cried to see that indomitable spirit which had carried her mother through so many of life's battles was doused. Her mind seemed to wander and from time to time she suffered from hallucinations.

Meanwhile, the 23rd Division, including Fred, arrived in Italy in early September 1917, and now progressed slowly towards the

Piave valley. The weather in the north of Italy was cold, and the terrain mountainous and arduous, but there was less mud than on the overworked battlefields of France, and fewer towns had been destroyed. Fred, who always had had an eye for architecture, greatly admired some of the buildings and sent Harriet postcards saying as much; of course the place names were obliterated by the censor. Through Fred's series of postcards to Harriet she realised he was in Italy, but had no real knowledge of his whereabouts. He had managed to see Adrienne and her family before he left for Italy; they exchanged home addresses and promised to write to each other when the war was over. He sent them a postcard from Italy and they, in return, sent him a New Year card, telling him that Watten had 20 centimetres of snow at the time, that they were all well and often thought of him. Fred also received a letter from George Henry, still serving in India, saying that he was well, but fed up with being away from home; he had had no home leave since being sent to Peshawar.

1918

William, in 1917, had been stationed on the Western Front twenty miles or so south of Ypres, but participated in fierce fighting at Ginchy, in October and November. His regiment then marched to Lagnicourt in December, where they encountered shelling until the fifteenth of the month. They spent Christmas week 1917 digging trenches for a support line behind Lagnicourt. On January 31st 1918 William was detailed to a night patrol in 'No Man's Land'. The crack of a German sniper's rifle rang out; the patrol dropped to the ground, and began to crawl back towards the trenches, except for William, who had been shot dead. His companions dragged his body back to the trenches as they crawled through the cover of the night.

Once again a letter from the Front brought news of a son's death. When Alice read Sarah the letter bringing the news of William's death, she was almost hysterical; she had lost her husband and two sons within six months. Harriet and Alice did the best they could to console their mother. Both feared for their respective husbands, while she still worried about her remaining son, George Henry. He wrote regularly to other family members, reassuring them that there were no battles in India, mainly drill and training other soldiers. Fred's letters from Italy were also reassuring, no more mud, as on the Somme and at Ypres. By October 1918, the men on the march in Italy knew that the war was all but over and the Allies had won. Fred sent Harriet a postcard on November 4th, guarding his words, he simply wrote 'What about the war?' At the eleventh hour of the eleventh day of the eleventh month of 1918, Fred and his unit were in Italy, and celebrated with a few bottles of red Italian wine. Harriet was ecstatic, imagining that Fred would be home by Christmas. Fred, knowing the immensity of organising troop transport, had no such illusions.

In the quiet of the evening, having a last smoke, while most of his companions had fallen asleep, Fred's thoughts returned to his home and his wish to have a child of his own. He thought of William, Harriet's brother, so handsome and charming, he could have had the pick of any of the girls in Bedminster. Instead, he had enlisted at twenty, been sent to the Front, and had been shot by a sniper only nine months before the war ended. Nothing of William left behind, only a weeping mother, wondering why she had nurtured a son all those years, to have him killed on a foreign field. And young Arthur, who had married his sweetheart, Elsie, before he went to war, to ensure she was waiting for him when he returned, blown to smithereens when he had only been at the Front a few months. Not even enough of him left to bury, they said, but they would put his name on a memorial after the war. Arthur was too young to have been sent abroad, they shouldn't have taken him, unless he lied about his age as so many others had. Fred remembered meeting Archie Palmer, a lad from Devon, in the first year of the war. He admitted to Fred, he was only fifteen then. He had enlisted at fourteen, and been 'over the top' three times before his fifteenth birthday. Their paths had crossed briefly; Fred wondered where he was now. George Henry, Harriet's eldest brother was still alive and well, as was Jim Budd, the husband of Harriet's sister, who had served in the Merchant Navy.

Fred thought of all the dead young men he had seen throughout the war; what a waste, he thought.

HARRIET'S FAMILY

William John Bolt, photo taken while on leave during The Great War. Shot by a sniper 1918.

WHEN THE WAR'S OVER......

Gradually the British troops were repatriated and discharged. Although there had seemed many jobs at home during the war, necessitating the employment of women, even when these jobs were ceded there was not enough work for the men returning from the Front. And yet far fewer men returned than had enlisted. Where had the jobs gone?

Commerce and industry had declined during the course of the War, as spending power lessened among those left at home. Everything was directed towards the war effort, and it seemed frivolous to think of buying anything that was not a necessity. At the end of hostilities, munitions factories closed and all their associated suppliers were suddenly without a market. Transport had been geared to war needs for four years; these were suddenly removed.

Women who had been cherished as important workers during the war suddenly found themselves unemployed with no redress. As a gesture of recognition of the importance of the role women had played during the war, the right to vote was given to married women and women who owned property.

'Looks as though poor women are being excluded again,' thought Harriet. 'Suppose they don't count still.'

Coming home from the War, after the initial euphoria of return, suddenly became the shock of reality. There were no jobs and there was no money. What a heroes' return, for some! George Henry was reinstated in his job at George's Brewery, and Alice's husband, Jim Budd, resumed his work at the factory. Ellen's husband Alfred returned safely and resumed work as a docker. Ellen thankfully reliquished her domestic job to become a full-time housewife, although Alf's pay as a docker was scarcely enough to keep them. Within a year of his return from the Army their daughter, Amy, was born.

Fred was one of the less fortunate. After his discharge on 30th of May 1919, and a brief 'settling-in' period at home, he returned to Murray's, to ask for his job back, which had been promised at enlistment. Sorry, he was told, we have no jobs for cabinetmakers, as we have no work. No one is buying furniture. If trade picks up, we will let you know. Many men, besides Fred, found that there was no redress against employers who had made empty promises of keeping jobs open, and there was no government assistance either.

He returned home to a disgruntled Harriet. Although the shop trade was improving, as more goods became available, it would not provide sufficient income for all of them. She had by this time used all the money awarded on the death of her first husband, this had been spent on the two girls, Alice was now twelve and Lilian nearly ten. Fred went in search of work, as did so many other ex-soldiers. There was no work in the Bristol area for a skilled carpenter, even as a fitter or carpenter on a building site.

As if that were not enough, a letter, in unfamiliar handwriting, with a French stamp and a French postmark, arrived addressed to Fred. It was from Adrienne, enquiring if Fred had reached home safely after the war. Fred's spoken French was rudimentary; it was with great difficulty he read and translated the letter to Harriet. She, of course, was furious, convinced this was a French mistress Fred had kept in France. Was this where their hard-earned money had been spent? The letter invited Fred and his family to France for a holiday, but Harriet would have none of it. She viewed foreign countries and foreigners with suspicion, and Adrienne with even greater suspicion—after all, the letter was in French, she only had Fred's word for the contents. There were strong words between Harriet and Fred, with the result that no more letters were exchanged and the relationship drew to an end.

Harriet felt hurt and betrayed; sacrifices she had made to send money to Fred, keeping the home together while working hard, and he had repaid her by carrying on with some French floozy. Fred felt injured and angry; he had not been unfaithful as had so many of his comrades during the war years, and who could blame them, Fred had thought. Facing death every day, coping with dreadful deprivations, sex was a welcome oblivion if only for a fleeting moment. But not for him. And Harriet refused to believe him; that hurt most of all. Through his relatives who still lived in London, Fred heard of a job fitting cinema seats. Having just returned from almost four years of enforced absence, Fred again had to leave his family in order to work and support them. In the light of the strained atmosphere at home, neither Fred nor Harriet viewed this as such an unwelcome event as might have been expected. He lodged with one of his uncles, and returned home as many weekends as he was able. One of his London relatives, Uncle Charles, had become a licensed taxi driver. Fred, with his Army driving experience, was an ideal candidate and worked initially part-time as a taxi driver, then full-time when the cinema contract ended. But he continued to look for work in Bristol and would combine his weekend visits home with job-seeking. Eventually his persistence was rewarded and he was offered a post on the maintenance staff with the Gas Board at Eastville in Bristol. The family was permanently reunited at last, and Harriet and Fred's relationship restored to its usual equable calm.

Chapter 6

FOUR FUNERALS AND A WEDDING

FRED SETTLED into his new job well; he usually rode his bicycle to work as it was quicker than taking the tram. One evening, as he stored his bike in the yard at the back of the shop he heard violent knocking on the side door. Harriet had only just closed the shop so Fred sighed, assuming it was a late customer, and opened the door to find Mabel's husband outside, in a very distressed state.

'Oh Fred, I'm so glad you're home,' his breath came in gasps. Fred drew him inside, alarmed at the man's condition and surprised to see him, as they were not close friends.

'What's the trouble? Take a deep breath. Do you want to sit down?'

'No, no, come at once, it's Mabel.'

Harriet, hearing the noise, had joined them from the kitchen, startled by her brother-in-law's agitation. Fred left without a word and Richard followed him while Harriet returned to the kitchen; the children were seated at the table as she was about to serve the evening meal.

'Daddy's gone to sort it out,' she consoled them as they were looking frightened. 'It will be all right. Now start your tea, I'll put Daddy's back in the oven.'

Fred was gone for some time, but Harriet was worried about leaving the children and could not eat her own meal. When they had finished eating she sent them upstairs to play and crossed the road to Mabel's house. There was a little knot of neighbours outside, and Fred came out and put his arm round her.

'You might not want to go in,' he said gently. 'Mabel is dead. She must have fallen down the stairs, I think her neck is broken.'

'Oh no, Fred, not Mabel.' Tears formed in Harriet's eyes.

As she spoke the doctor arrived and pushed past the gawpers. Harriet followed him into the house and there was Mabel, lying at the bottom of the stairs with her head at a strange angle. Wiping her tears Harriet watched as he carried out his examination; she felt it was only right there should be another woman present. He pronounced her dead, and began asking Richard questions. Realising there was nothing she could do, Harriet returned home to look to her daughters, leaving Fred to assist Richard.

It was some time later that evening when Fred returned. He had invited Richard to return with him, but the unhappy man wished to stay at home. Mabel's body had been taken to the hospital for post-mortem.

'The doctor is pretty certain that was what killed her, but they've got to be certain,' he said. 'The funny thing was, she was obviously dressed to go out, and she had almost a thousand pounds in her handbag.'

'What!' exclaimed Harriet. 'Where did she get that sort of money? And where was she going with it?'

'I've no idea, and neither has Richard,' Fred replied, 'unless someone else comes up with a reason it's going to be one of life's unsolved mysteries. Anyway, I must go and see my mother and father, to let them know. I'll call at Charles' on the way past, and he can go and tell Maud and then Uriah.'

'Your tea's in the oven, you ought to have something to eat before you go, Fred.'

'I couldn't at the moment, dear, perhaps later,' and he was gone.

They sat together on the sofa later that evening and shed a few tears together. Poor Mabel, she had not had an especially happy life, with a husband who did not appreciate her, and no children. 'Makes you count your blessings, doesn't it?' said Harriet. Fred, usually undemonstrative, kissed her.

Shortly after Fred's return from London Harriet realised she was pregnant. Fred was delighted; this was to be the child he had dreamed of, sitting on the cold, wet battlefields of war. Both hoped for a son, Harriet because she already had two daughters, and Fred because he wanted a son to carry on his name. In fact they had conceived a son, as was confirmed by the doctor who attended Harriet's miscarriage.

'I am sorry, but there will be other sons,' he told Harriet, meaning to be kind. 'You are still young.'

'But I don't want to wear myself out having child after child, miscarriage after miscarriage, like my mother,' thought Harriet. 'I'm thirty-four now; so just one more try.'

In the January of 1920 Harriet conceived again, and Fred treated her like porcelain china. She still looked after the shop, but Fred insisted she sat behind the counter, rather than standing. Fred did the shop figures at the weekend (although Harriet still checked them). The girls, Alice and Lilian, restocked shelves in the evenings and visited the wholesalers on Saturday mornings. When Alice commenced working at the Wills tobacco factory, the bulk of the shop work fell to Lilian, after school and at weekends. Lilian disliked the tasks associated with the shop, especially the Saturday morning trips to the wholesalers. Harriet insisted these were undertaken early in the morning; there were no more Saturday lie-ins for Lilian.

It was during Harriet's pregnancy that Ellen brought the news that her stepmother, Martha Fricker, had died. Harriet was upset, as she had loved Martha, who had been so kind to her during her marriage to Bill, but Fred would not hear of her travelling to South Wales for the funeral. Harriet offered to look after one-year-old Amy for the day; as the funeral was on Sunday she could manage the shop and the little girl. Ellen and her husband travelled to South Wales with her brother George and his wife, Saranne.

In September Harriet's daughter was born, and named Edna Grace; traditions had changed and children were no longer expected to be named after other family members. Harriet was relieved to have safely delivered her baby, and not too disappointed not to have a son; Fred was delighted to have a child of his own, with fair hair and blue eyes like him.

'She was worth waiting for, Harriet,' he said. 'I've never told you before, but when I was in France and I got the news that young Arthur was killed, I thought, well, poor chap. Gone, and left nothing behind him, not a child, nothing, just as though he'd never been. Then I thought, that could be me too; although I love Alice and Lil like my own, they don't carry anything of me in them. It made me extra careful to make sure I got home safely.'

'Thank God you did come back safe Fred, for your own sake, but it is good to have our child.'

Alice and Lilian were delighted with their baby sister, if a little jealous of all the attention she merited, not only from their parents, but other relatives, friends and shop customers. There was a gap of eleven years between Lilian and Edna; a baby in the family after all that time deserved a welcome.

Harriet once again took over the reins of the family shop. Little Edna was fitted in with shop duties, as Harriet had seen her own mother manage baby Arthur and the family shop twenty years ago—except that there had also been George Henry as a full-time worker. Lilian helped in the shop after school but without enthusiasm. Harriet's shop in Bloy Street was not as busy as the family's Bedminster shop had been; Harriet determined the shop would 'tick over' not expand while she had a young baby. As Edna grew and became more active Harriet decided she either needed help in the shop or help with her domestic duties.

She decided to discuss the idea with Fred one evening.

'I am finding the shop, the baby and the housework too much for one person, Fred,' she began, 'and I was wondering whether to

take on some help, either with the shop or with the house, perhaps someone who would look after Edna as well when I'm busy.'
'Well don't tire yourself out,' Fred was immediately anxious.
'Perhaps you should give up the shop altogether.'
'Oh no, that's not necessary. After all, Edna will only be little for a few years, but I want to make sure she's not neglected while she is an infant.'
'Would you rather have someone to help with the shop?' asked Fred.
'Not if I can find someone reliable to come here and mind Edna, so I can keep an eye on them. I won't have her going to someone else's house to be looked after.'
'You do what you think best, dear,' said Fred, knowing full well that Harriet would.

Harriet was certain that domestic help was the better option. She decided she would pay for as much domestic help as she needed, provided she still showed a profit against the shop takings and made enquiries of customers whether they knew of a reliable childminder. Mrs Powell was recommended by a neighbour; she had a son the same age as Edna and would bring him with her, so the two children could play together. She was also willing to incorporate a little housework into her duties, which relieved Harriet of the constant tiredness she had felt since the baby's birth. The family's 'heavy' washing was taken by a neighbour, who took in washing for a living. Harriet began to feel that her life was returning to normal; even if the shop profits were depleted for a few years it would be worth it, she reasoned.

Shortly before Edna was born Harriet's sister had confided that she too was pregnant, and hoping for a son, as she also had two daughters. Early in 1921 her daughter, Ivy, was born, but unlike Fred, Alice's husband was supremely disinterested in his third daughter. Alice was also experiencing problems with their mother, Sarah, who still lived with her. The old lady was exhibiting some strange behaviour - such as pulling out all her teeth. Harriet visited her mother as often as she could, but could offer little practical help to Alice.

Early the following year Alice called the doctor to their mother as she seemed to be very short of breath and found great difficulty in even climbing the stairs.

'He says it's heart disease, there's nothing he can do. Probably the valves of her heart are just worn out,' Alice told Harriet.

'I wish there was something I could do,' said Harriet. 'Shall I come on Wednesday afternoon and sit with her?'

'I'm sure she would like that,' Alice replied, 'though she's not bed-bound yet.'

Each week Harriet took Edna and spent Wednesday afternoon with her mother. It gave Alice the opportunity to spend time with Ivy, away from the care of her mother. Harriet could see that Sarah was declining fast. The fifth week she suggested that Alice call Dr Kerfoot again, as her mother seemed generally unwell.

'Dr Kerfoot said he thought she had an infection and gave her some medicine,' Alice told Harriet the following Sunday, when Harriet made an extra visit, 'but she's no better.'

Harriet visited again on Wednesday, leaving Edna with Mrs Powell, as she felt the sickroom was no place for a two-year-old. Her mother was very ill and died the next day. There was no need for a post-mortem, said Dr Kerfoot, as he had seen her several times within the past few weeks.

Both daughters, but especially Alice, felt the stress of invalid-care lifting, but both mourned the woman who had loved them, provided them with a home and taught them to be independent, in spite of the hard life she had experienced herself. Before the lid was placed on the coffin Harriet kissed her mother's cold cheek. 'Goodbye, Ma, you have been a wonderful mother,' she whispered, 'thank you for all you've taught me.' Alice, standing silently in the doorway, felt a tear roll down her cheek.

A woman not mourned by Harriet was her mother-in-law, who died about the same time as her own mother. Fred and his brothers organised the funeral. None of Mrs Lewis's daughters-in-law

HARRIET'S FAMILY

wanted to attend, as she had made enemies of all of them.

'If I go to the funeral I shall dance on her grave,' declared Charles' wife, Clara. Even Harriet did not feel quite this vehement and certainly would not have said so in Fred's presence. In fact, Clara made her feelings known by sporting a red feather in the black hat she wore to the funeral, which scandalised a number of neighbours and relatives. Uriah's wife said nothing, but opened another bottle, in which she was increasingly finding solace these days. When Uriah returned from the funeral he found her face down in the vegetable garden, drunk and unconscious. It had begun to rain, as so often on funeral days, so Uriah left her there for the rain to sober her.

Fred's father had sold his shops several years previously, and after the death of his wife, he sold his house and went to live with his youngest daughter, Elvina, and her husband. No one quite knew what happened to Isaac's money, but a few years later he had a young ladyfriend, upon whom he lavished gifts, fur coats, handmade boots and jewellery. His sons and daughters were scandalised, but Isaac ignored them. Even Elvina, who provided him with a home, could not make him see he was being foolish—if foolish he was. Isaac was happy in his own way, possibly happier than he had been before, and continued to live a long and happy life.

Life became humdrum but contented for Harriet and her family. Lilian had left school and started work at Packer's, a local chocolate factory. Fred took great delight in watching his daughter growing up and although he never really liked work, he now had a purpose. Harriet still closed the shop for a half-day on Wednesdays, when she either visited her sister or went to Mothers' Union meetings, taking Edna with her. Fred's sister, Maud, by now had three daughters, two of whom were at school. She was a leading light in Mothers' Union, being responsible for making tea. She always slipped Edna an extra biscuit; Edna liked Auntie Maud. Because Edna was a slight little thing, everyone assumed she needed feeding, but on the contrary, she had a good appetite and ate well. There was no shortage of food in the Lewis household, especially as it came at cost-price.

The post-war decline of Bristol Docks meant that steady work for the men was not available, so Ellen's husband took any work he could find, often working as an agricultural labourer on the farms around Bristol, with even worse than dock-labour. Some of the dockers were travelling to Southampton where there was more work available than in Bristol, and staying for a week or a month or until the work ran out. Alfred decided he would join them and it was during his stay in Southampton, while unloading a shipment of fruit from Africa, that he was bitten by an insect and was later found to have contracted sleeping sickness. He died within eighteen months; Amy was four years old when he died.

Ellen was already renting the cheapest cottage she could find, one room upstairs, one room down; Harriet was horrified at the state of it.

'You don't even have proper stairs!' she said. 'It's more like a ladder to go up to the bedroom.'

Ellen was adamant she would live frugally. She did small housecleaning jobs, taking Amy with her, and usually managed to pay her rent and buy food, but when winter came and they needed fuel as well, life became more difficult. Ellen swallowed her pride, and taking Amy by the hand she went to the Poor Law Commissioners to ask for financial help. She explained her circumstances, that she could finance her rent and food, but the purchase of a few bags of coal was beyond her means. The commissioners conferred, then one spoke to her.

'Do you have any furniture in your house, Mrs Evans?' he asked. Ellen frowned, puzzled.

'Well, yes,' she said. 'A bed, table and chairs, a cupboard.'

'Well then,' the commissioner replied, 'we suggest that you go home and chop up some furniture to light a fire. In the meantime, we are willing to give you half a loaf of bread a day, if you would like to call at side door for it.'

Ellen was horrified; this was not what she wanted. She rose to her feet, wrapped her shawl around her and took Amy by the hand.

'I asked for coal not half a loaf of bread. I suggest you keep it,' she retorted and swept out of the room.

Harriet was delighted when Ellen told her this story.

'Well done, why should you be treated like dirt? It's no fault of yours that your husband died.' Harriet thought of her own experiences after Bill's death. 'These wretched Boards and Commissioners think they know just how we live and what we ought to do. It needs someone to stand up to them. It needs a change in the Law. Now, how will you manage? Is there anything I can do to help?'

Resourceful as ever, Ellen decided it was time to return to work full time; she managed to find a post as cook-housekeeper to a doctor's family, in Stackpole Road, where she could take Amy with her, explaining that in another six months the child would be at school. Ellen and Amy had a warm environment, adequate food and an employer who appreciated Ellen's capabilities, as she was a very good cook.

Harriet's sister's baby was due. 'One final attempt to have a son,' she told Harriet, and sure enough, a son was born. Ronald Henry James, born when Ivy was three, was a happy healthy baby. Alice and Jim were delighted with their son; all three of his sisters adored him. The following winter, however, Ronnie developed bronchitis and died, age 9 months. Once again Alice and Harriet cried together.

'We are obviously not meant to have sons,' Harriet said. Jim distanced himself psychologically from his family of women; it marked a permanent change in Alice and Jim's relationship.

When Edna was five years old she started at the local school. Mrs Powell, who was escorting her own son to the same school each morning, called for Edna, and collected both children after school. One afternoon Edna decided she simply had to go to the toilet before she walked home. The toilets were in a separate building, in the school playground. Many of the children—girls as well as boys—thought it very funny to run past the toilet block pushing all the doors open as they ran, exposing the unfortunate incumbents sitting on the toilet, so Edna carefully locked the door behind her. When she tried to unlock the door it would not budge. The door was a solid door, with no gap top or bottom and full height partitions between each toilet, to ensure privacy, a prison. After several tries, she resorted to banging on the door and shouting for help, but all her schoolfriends had gone home by that time. She slid to the cold stone floor, sobbing, convinced she was there for the night if not forever. The caretaker, on his rounds, did not hear her, and went into the school building. Mrs Powell followed him in, to enquire whether Edna had been kept behind for some reason.

'Oh no,' said her teacher, 'she left at the same time as all the others. Perhaps her mother or sister collected her.'

Mrs Powell thought this highly unlikely, but there was no sign of Edna in the school building. She went directly to Harriet's shop, to ask whether anyone else had collected the child. Harriet was distraught, imagining kidnap and worse. She shut the shop immediately and ran to the school, where she insisted that the caretaker search all the rooms. Suddenly he thought of the toilet block. As they crossed the playground the winter afternoon was getting dark; the building was silent, but they pushed all the doors open—except one, which was locked from the inside.

'Edna, are you in there?' called Harriet. A tiny whimper was all they heard. The caretaker fetched a crowbar and forced the door open. Tiny Edna was curled into a ball at the back of the toilet, her fists pressed against her mouth, uttering indistinct sobs. She was so distressed she could not move. Harriet lifted her gently and consoled her as they walked home.

'Don't ever lock the lavvy door again,' Harriet instructed. I won't, thought Edna, and it was a very long time before she was able to bring herself to lock any door behind her.

The family enjoyed simple pleasures, days out at the seaside, family picnics in nearby countryside. Alice, now age twenty, and Lilian, going on eighteen, considered themselves too old and sophisticated for these simple pursuits, so outings usually comprised Harriet, Fred and Edna and occasionally they took Alice's daughter, Ivy. Edna loved the wild flowers; moon daisies and bluebells especially. She picked handfulls to give to Harriet.

'They won't last in water, Edna, they are wild and need to stay in the wild,' she told the child, who understood but still had the compulsion to take some of the countryside home. It was partly that Fred realised he and Edna would love to have a garden, and partly that Harriet, now past forty, was beginning to tire of running the shop, that they decided to sell the business and buy a house in nearby St George. The house they chose had a garden and was near St George's park.

It was a good solid Edwardian house, with a bay-windowed front parlour and three bedrooms. There was a small front garden and a larger garden at the rear, so Fred could grow flowers and vegetables once again. Edna was seven years old by this time, and had to change schools, but effected the change with no problems. Both Alice and Lilian had to take the tram to work. Fred, too, began to find the tram an easier option than cycling.

Alice and Lilian had enjoyed dancing; they were adept at The Charleston and other modern dances of the day. Harriet's eyes widened but she only said 'you be careful, my girl, it looks very flighty.' Privately she thought, how times had changed, it would never have been allowed when she was a girl. About the time they moved house, Alice met a young man at a dance; his name was Reg Thomas, and he also lived in St George; a serious courtship ensued.

They married in 1928. Alice wore a white dress, as 'everyone wears white for their weddings nowadays' and wore a fashionable beaded cap with her veil. She was attended by a retinue of bridesmaids, including her two sisters. In all it was an elaborate wedding, a far cry Harriet thought from either of her own weddings. She was pleased that they were able to afford to give their eldest daughter the type of wedding she wanted. The happy couple went to live with Reg's parents who had spare rooms available, as their other children had already married and left home. They rented a living room and bedroom and shared the bathroom and kitchen with Reg's parents. Lilian missed her constant companion and confidant, but was delighted to have a bedroom to herself, for the first time in her life.

Just over a year later Alice and Reg had a son; Harriet found vicarious pleasure in her daughter's son. Unfortunately Reg's mother was not so pleased, as baby Ken cried a great deal. Even when Alice and her baby were in their own rooms, if Ken cried, Mrs Thomas would bang on the door and shout

'Can't you keep that baby quiet? Is there to be no peace?'

Consequently each day Alice had the choice of either nursing the baby all day, to prevent him crying, or wheeling him in his pram to her mother's, taking her washing with her. Then either she or Harriet would do the washing, in Harriet's sink, whilst the other nursed the baby. Harriet felt that Alice and Reg needed a home of their own. She and Fred had also discussed moving house again; they did not like St George as much as they had anticipated and were also having trouble with the neighbours. When they first moved into the house the nextdoor neighbour, Bella, had appeared very friendly. Gradually she had changed her attitude to one of animosity; one of the triggers was Harriet's parrot. When they were leaving the shop a customer who was unable to settle her account gave Harriet the parrot in lieu of payment. The bird already had a fine vocabulary and could utter a number of phrases. On fine days Harriet would hang the parrot's cage in the back garden for the bird to have some fresh air. Whenever Bella appeared in her adjoining garden, the bird saw it as a cue to utter a string of words and phrases, the favourite being 'Get out of here'.

Bella took exception to this.

'I won't be told to get out of my own garden!' she shouted. Harriet tried to explain that the bird did not understand what it was saying, but Bella would have none of it.

'How come he always shouts that at me then?' she asked. Harriet had no answer to this; for some reason the bird associated that phrase with Bella. Eventually relationships between the two women became very strained.

Fred told Harriet about some new houses being built near his place of work '- not far from Eastville Park, where we used to go for walks during the wartime,' he enthused. 'They are well-spaced out, with big gardens, especially the one on the corner plot.' Harriet went to see the site, discussed the plans with the builder and they put down a deposit on the new house. They planned to retain their house in St George and rent it to tenants. 'The rent will pay off the loan on our new house and we shall eventually own two houses outright,' Harriet planned. There were some cheaper houses being built at the far end of the road, needing a smaller deposit, which Alice and Reg decided would be an ideal first home for them.

Chapter 7

FOUR WEDDINGS AND A FUNERAL

In 1931 Harriet, Fred, Lilian and Edna moved into their new house, 7 Heath Road, Eastville. The new housing in the area was part of the expansion of towns and cities into the 'suburbs', a plan inaugurated by Wheatley in 1924 to provide two and a half million new homes by 1939. The house was a brick-built pebbled dashed semi, with bay windows upstairs and down, making the house much lighter than the Victorian and Edwardian houses Harriet had previously occupied. She loved her new house; the windows opened easily, compared to the old sash windows, and all the plumbing and wiring was neatly concealed in the walls. Harriet arranged and rearranged her furniture and ornaments to suit the new house, altering curtains to fit and making new ones. But there was no longer any need to crochet new mantlepiece covers or make drapes for the piano legs, these were no longer in fashion.

Harriet's sister, Alice, came to see the house, bringing her youngest daughter, Ivy. Harriet thought she detected envy in her sister's eyes, but young Ivy frankly fell in love with the house. She became a frequent weekend visitor, being only a year younger than Edna the two girls were company for each other, which helped Edna settle into her new environment.

As with their previous house at St George, this house had three bedrooms, so Lilian and Edna had a room each. There was a front parlour housing the piano, china cabinet and a new overstuffed velour three-piece; this room was kept locked, in the old Victorian tradition, with the key on the top of the doorframe. The living room was at the back of the house, as was the kitchen, which Harriet had persuaded the builder to extend to twice the size on the plans, so as to include a breakfast room.

Fred could walk to work at the Gas Works in five minutes, which left him plenty of time and energy to start converting a building site to the garden of his dreams. He laid paved steps and paths at the front of the house, edged with flowerbeds, and cut stout sticks from trees along the riverbank to make a trellis for rambling roses. The back garden boasted a small lawn and a vegetable patch. Snails were carefully collected and cooked, rather than squashed, a relic of Fred's sojourn in France.

'I'm not eating those,' Harriet declared.

'Neither am I,' added Lilian.

'All the more for you and I then, Edna,' said Fred.

Young Edna ate them readily, although she did not share her father's passion for rare beef or solid rice pudding.

Freed from the constraints of opening a shop fifty-two weeks of the year, and with the introduction of paid leave for holidays by Fred's employer, Harriet and Fred were able to indulge their passion for seaside holidays. Harriet had always loved the seaside; with the advent of the railways enabling daytrips to the coast she had frequently taken the opportunity of visits to Weston-super-Mare or Weymouth on Bank Holidays. Now the family could spend a whole week at the seaside, with the exception of Lilian, who did not have paid holidays. Full board was booked at a private boarding house at Weymouth each year, new clothes were purchased specifically for the holidays, not only for Harriet and Edna. Fred became debonair in new grey flannels, a sports coat and new flat cap to wear for a stroll along the Prom. The boarding house meals consisted of breakfast, lunch and high tea each day, so fish and chip suppers were eaten several times during the week; Weymouth's fish and chips were highly regarded by Fred, who was something of a connoisseur.

Edna had started piano lessons a year before the house move; a new piano teacher had to be found for her, as well as a new school. The school transition was a success, but the piano teacher used such different methods from her previous one that Edna could not cope and gave up music. The following month Edna was due to take her 'eleven-plus'—the public exam determining whether Edna moved on to a grammar school or a secondary modern. She had passed the mock-exam a week earlier with flying colours.

Harriet was concerned that academic work at a grammar school might be too much for Edna. In addition, if they had still lived at St George, the Grammar School was nearby, but from their new house Edna would have too far to walk and would need to catch two buses to school, whereas the secondary modern school was within easy walking distance. Neither of her other daughters had attended Grammar schools, and both had subsequently found reasonable jobs. Anyway, Edna was such a pretty girl she was sure to get married and leave work, so she would have no need of a career. Harriet forgot her own circumstances, when she was left a widow with no means of support when a career would have been a lifeline.

Edna solved Harriet's dilemma by developing flu on the day of the exam, and was much too ill to attend school for several weeks. Harriet visited the school to ask whether Edna might take the exam at a later date, but was told this was not possible.

Edna was upset to think that she would not be attending the Grammar School, but as her mother did not seem to think it was a problem she adjusted her mindset and commenced her three years at Eastville Girls' School, with a number of her friends.

Lilian had grown into a tall, elegant young woman; she was taller than either Harriet or Fred. Of course, her father was tall, Harriet thought, she must take after him. Lilian had met a young man, who was paying her constant attention; eventually Tom Brommage asked for Lilian's hand in marriage. He was a tall, personable young man, a stone mason by trade, who was working on renovations to St Mary Redcliffe Church.

'That's interesting,' said Fred, 'my father worked on the previous restoration when he first came to Bristol, must have been in the eighteen-seventies. He was a stone mason too, in those days.'

Lilian and Tom were married on Boxing Day, 1932, at the local parish church, Holy Trinity in Stapleton, with Edna and her cousin Ivy as bridesmaids together with Tom's only sister, Peggy. Ivy's sister Rose also wanted the girls to be bridesmaids at her wedding, which was to take place the following month.

'Oh dear,' said Harriet, 'you girls be careful; they say "three times a bridesmaid, never a bride" and that would be the third time for each of you.'

'Nonsense, Ma,' retorted Edna with a shake of her head, and Ivy giggled. 'We shall be bridesmaids lots more times yet; Ivy has another sister who will probably get married soon—we are very much in demand.'

Tom and Lilian went to live in a small Victorian terraced house in Saxon Road, St Werburghs, near Tom's parents; this was the street where Ernie Bevin had lived with his wife, until his call to London's political scene. The following Christmas baby Joyce was born; Lilian found she had her hands full.

'How you ever managed to run the shop when Edna was a baby, I don't know,' she confided to her mother. 'I don't seem to have a minute to myself.'

'It comes with practice,' Harriet replied, but remembered how constantly tired she had felt.

Fred, Edna and Harriet, on a family holiday at Weymouth, circa 1934.

Eight months after Lilian's baby was born Edna was fourteen and due to leave school. She told her mother and father she wanted to be a nurse.

'That's a very hard profession, long hours, lots of dirty work,' Harriet said, looking at her tiny, slightly-built daughter, who appeared even more fragile due to her cloud of blonde hair and blue eyes. 'Besides, you have to be more than fourteen to take up nursing. You would have to find something else to do for at least three years, if not four.'

'There's nothing else I really want to do,' Edna replied.

'The hairdresser's at Eastville are advertising in their window for an apprentice; that would be three years. How about applying for that?'

Edna duly applied for the apprenticeship and was given the job; Fred and Harriet paid her premium. She found that hairdressing was hard work and long hours, working a six-day week, frequently not finishing before seven o'clock in the evening. She was a willing worker, showed an aptitude for the job and was happy to take on responsibility. Within eighteen months she was responsible for ordering the stock for the shop, and frequently left to lock up the premises at night and open them next day.

Harriet was pleased that her daughter had taken so well to her work, and had made a wide circle of friends. Edna and her friends went to a dance one evening, when one of them introduced her to a young man in his twenties, Lawrence Kent, who was an excellent dancer. Edna enjoyed dancing and had a good sense of rhythm so they were a good partnership. During one of the intervals Lawrence was saying that he needed to find new lodgings, as his landlady and her husband were constantly quarrelling, which made him feel uncomfortable. He looked directly at Edna.

'Does your mother take in lodgers? '

'No,' replied Edna, 'that's something she's never done. We do have a spare room now my sister's married, but I don't think Ma will want to let it.'

'Will you ask her for me?' asked Lawrence. 'I'm really keen to move.'

Edna forgot about the conversation and went to work next day without mentioning it to Harriet. When she came home after work she was astounded to see Lawrence Kent sitting at the kitchen table talking to her mother, having decided to come and ask Harriet for himself! He was a polite and charming young man, and had succeeded in charming Harriet into saying that he could move in as a lodger the following week.

'But,' said Harriet, direct as always, 'this is on the understanding that there is nothing but friendship between you and Edna; otherwise this is not going to work. It has to be a business relationship.'

'On my honour, Mrs Lewis,' Lawrence said and shook hands. Within a month he had dropped the 'Mrs Lewis' and was calling Harriet 'Ma'.

Harriet took happily to having a lodger; she enjoyed cooking and looking after people. Lawrence was very appreciative as Harriet was a good cook; he often said that his previous landlady couldn't even cook toast.

'Ma,' he said one day, on his return from work, 'there's a new chap started work with us who doesn't have anywhere to live. How about he has the other single bed in my room?'

Lodgers sharing rooms were commonplace at that time, and so Charlie came to join the family too. He was older than Lawrence and had a bald head, a feature which Lawrence frequently indicated by treating Charlie's head as a drum, tapping out rhythms on it. Sometimes Charlie retaliated but it was impossible to be angry with Lawrence for long, he was such a bubbly personality. He loved music and dancing; when there was a dance tune on the radio he would catch Harriet or Edna by the waist and whirl them round the kitchen.

'Lawrence, you are a fool,' Harriet would protest, 'you are going to knock something over. Be careful.'

'There's no need for you to do all this extra work, dear' Fred said to her, as she was plating five meals in the kitchen one evening. 'We don't need the money that badly.'

'In a way I'm quite enjoying it,' Harriet replied, 'they are like the sons we never had.'

Alice and Reg, having moved into their house at the end of Heath Road, had also taken a lodger. Amy, Ellen's daughter, had a new job at the Aircraft factory and needed to live near the bus route to work. As a lodger she was ideal, easy to please and willing to babysit with young Ken when needed.

In addition Harriet saw her 'job' as insurance against any of her family becoming unemployed as there were many businesses collapsing during the Depression in the nineteen-thirties. Bristol was not affected as badly as the industrial areas in the north-east, or South Wales—those very areas which had suffered worst during the General Strike in 1926 and its aftermath. But there were dole queues in Bristol, and Harriet, passing them on shopping expeditions, felt very sorry for those blank eyes staring unseeingly at the shabby queue ahead of them.

'I don't understand it, we're not at war now, why are things so bad?' she asked Fred.

'The problem is that none of the governments we have had since the war have been able to get to grips with the economy,' Fred replied. 'They keep using short term measures, like the year's subsidy given to mines in 1925; when it comes to an end, the big black hole is still there. And they can't seem to get unemployment down below one million.'

In fact there had been nearly four million unemployed in Britain in 1932, and six million in Germany. The economic problems of Britain were reflections of crises in other parts of the world, which meant that Britain's export markets were shrinking, and the financial policies which hampered exports had not been addressed. Some commentators wondered why the situation had not become more explosive. The Jarrow marchers, in 1936, drew attention to their plight, but even then the mood was not aggressive, as though all militancy had been exhausted after 1918.

'We are very lucky that we've all got jobs, you, the girls' husbands, the lodgers, even Edna.' Once again Harriet was counting her blessings.

Edna meanwhile had found a young man—or to be more precise, he had found her. She had been walking home from work one evening when a young man on a bicycle stopped beside her and asked her to go to the cinema with him.

'I don't know,' said Edna doubtfully. 'I don't know you at all.'

'I see you every evening,' said Len, 'I pass you on my bike on the way home from work. I live just up the road here, the one with the green front door, on the other side. My name is Len Rossiter.'

'Well, all right,' Edna was persuaded. He did look a nice young man, with very dark hair and hazel eyes. They arranged to meet at the cinema the following evening. Edna was surprised to find Len waiting outside the hairdresser's with his bicycle when she left work next day. She thought he was waiting to tell her he couldn't come to the cinema.

'I just thought I'd walk part of the way home with you,' Len said. 'My tea's not ready yet, so I have a bit of spare time.' In fact he walked all the way home with Edna, then jumped on his bike to ride home, calling out, 'See you at seven.'

'Who was that?' asked Harriet, who happened to catch sight of Len from the front bedroom window.

'His name's Len, I told you about him yesterday. We are going to the pictures tonight. He seems very nice but I don't know why he had to walk all the way home from work with me, if we are seeing each other later.'

Harriet laughed. 'That's to make sure of where you live, then if you didn't turn up he could come and fetch you. He must be keen, Edna.'

Edna was sixteen when she met Len. He was four years older than her and was completing an engineering apprenticeship. Within eighteen months they were engaged, Len had finished his apprenticeship and found a new job at the Bristol Aircraft Company at Filton. One June evening Edna and Len were just leaving to go to a dance when the doorbell rang; it was Ellen.

'Don't usually see you on an evening, come in,' said Harriet. 'Our Edna and Len are just off to a dance; I think your Amy is going with them. Fred and I were going to have a cup of tea, would you like one?'

'No, not for me, Harriet, I'm not stopping. I thought I ought to come in and let you know, my father died a few days ago, George received a letter from one of the boys.' Ellen had lived with George and Saranne for several years now their children had all left home. 'The funeral is in South Wales on Friday. We shall all be going, I don't know if you would like to come too.'

'Oh my dear, I am sorry, but he was a good age, he must be eighty-three by now. Do come in and have a cup of tea,' Harriet drew Ellen into the kitchen and put the kettle on. Fred was called and after a brief discussion it was decided that Harriet would go to old Mr Fricker's funeral with Ellen, George and Saranne.

'It's not till the afternoon, so we can get a train from Temple Meads in the morning,' Ellen said. 'Gilbert said there's room for all of us to stay the night there, so we don't have to travel back same day.'

On the way to Crumlin Harriet, Ellen, George and Saranne reminisced about old Mr Fricker.

'Remember how he used to keep moving house?' Ellen said. 'Once he got to South Wales he seemed to lose that wanderlust. He was very happy there.'

'Ah he liked the mine there,' added George, who had worked in mining all his life and was due to retire in four years time. 'Father was promoted well up the ladder there. He was a very popular man in the community, pillar of the chapel and all that.'

'Gilbert and the others who moved over there with him all stayed in South Wales, didn't they?' Harriet asked. She had not been to visit the relatives in South Wales for many years; having her shop and then her extending family had occupied all her time, but she had kept in touch by sending postcards from time to time. William Fricker senior was interred at Abercarn Cemetery. The funeral went as well as could be expected; it did not rain, as many had thought. Afterwards the family returned to Gilbert's house to partake of ham salad, cake and tea. There was no alcohol as the family and most of the neighbours were Chapel and teetotal. As the evening began to darken Harriet noticed many of the men slipping away in ones and twos. She made no comment, but wondered whether they were quietly going to find some stronger drinks; her own family's funerals usually supplied alcohol. She was wrong. Gilbert's wife, looking out of the window, said, 'Looks as though they're ready now, we had better all go outside.'

On the hillside opposite small lights were beginning to twinkle, one by one; they were the lights of the miners' pit-helmets. As they watched, the voices struck up in harmony; Harriet was entranced.

'Bread of heaven, bread of heaven,
Feed me till I want no more
Want no more –'

echoed around the valley. Tears rolled down Harriet's cheeks; she looked at Ellen whose cheeks were also wet with tears.

Harriet described the scene to Fred and Edna next day, when she returned home. 'There's nothing like a Welsh male voice choir,' said Fred, who had a keen appreciation of music and relished visits to the opera whenever he was in London. Harriet preferred music-hall songs and the hymns of her younger days, she and Fred never went to church, yet during her first marriage she and Will attended chapel regularly.

Towards the end of 1937 Edna and Len became engaged; to celebrate their engagement Len had organised an aeroplane trip for the two of them from Bristol to Cardiff, and a day-out ticket to the funfair at Barry Island. This generated a great deal of excitement within the family as none of the others had even considered flying. Harriet was very worried and said so to Fred, who tried to reassure her how safe they were. He had seen aircraft in use in the war and told her none had ever crashed unless they were shot down. 'And no one's going to be shooting at them these days,' he added.

The aircraft was a small biplane carrying six passengers and two crew. The passengers were issued with a small box containing cotton wool to put in their ears, and a piece of chewing gum. Edna was thrilled with the flight and her day at the funfair. The couple returned by train from Cardiff, to Stapleton Road station at Eastville. As they walked back from the station to Edna's home they saw Fred, leaning against a shop doorway puffing his pipe. 'Back safe and sound then?' he smiled. 'Had a good time?' Edna guessed he had been waiting to see them return; although he had not expressed anxiety she was sure he had been a little worried.

'It was wonderful, dad.'

Len laughed. 'She enjoyed it so much she wanted to come back by plane too, but I couldn't afford it.'

Edna told her mother how exciting the flight had been. 'You can't imagine flying over the streets, looking down on the houses and fields, and then we flew over the Bristol Channel where all you could see was water and the Welsh hills on the horizon.' Harriet shuddered at the thought, nothing would convince her to fly.

During the second half of 1938 world events began to infiltrate the family's thoughts. The previous year one of Edna's friends, Jimmy, had just returned early from what should have been a postgraduate year in Germany.

'Jimmy says the Germans are preparing for war,' Edna had told her father one evening.

'Nonsense,' her father replied. 'They wouldn't want war again, no more than this country would.' He needed to believe that The Great War was the 'war to end all wars', that his comrades sacrifices had not been in vain. Harriet was not so sure. 'People have very short memories,' she said.

Len was quite perturbed about the possibility of war. He had no expectations of being sent to fight, as his job, making aircraft, would obviously be essential during a war, but he saw the wider picture. He also had little faith in Mr Chamberlain.

The demands made by Germany of the Czech government during the summer of 1938 brought Europe to the brink of war to the extent that France mobilised her reservists. Chamberlain went to Munich to pursue his 'policy of appeasement' and Czechoslovakia was convinced to acquiesce to German requests. Chamberlain assumed that once Germany's demands and grievances were addressed, they would behave reasonably and peacefully. Winston Churchill did not agree.

Len thought that Chamberlain was wrong; he was either misled by Hitler, and therefore very gullible, or he was cynically buying time for Britain to prepare for war at the expense of other European countries.

'Maybe we should think about getting married sooner, rather than later,' he suggested to Edna. 'Think about it, then we'll discuss it with your parents.'

'What about your parents?' asked Edna. She had met Mr and Mrs Rossiter several times and thought they were very pleasant.

'I'm over twenty-one, dear, so it's my decision, not theirs,' Len replied, and Edna sensed some friction between Len and his parents. She wondered whether this might have some bearing on Len's wish to advance the date of the wedding, but she said nothing. She was quite happy to get married; Len was the man she wanted as a husband. He was hard-working, steady, affectionate—pity he was not a better dancer, but you can't have everything.

After family discussions it was decided to bring Edna and Len's wedding forward to September. Harriet's niece, Violet, was to be married in August; once again Ivy and Edna would be bridesmaids. Violet offered to loan Edna her wedding veil afterwards, as her 'something borrowed' item. Ivy and Amy were to be Edna's bridesmaids.

'All the experienced bridesmaids will be gone soon—who will you have, Ivy?' Edna quipped.

Harriet was a very proud mother on her daughter's wedding day; her pretty, blonde daughter looked lovely, she thought, in her white satin dress. Harriet's sister, Alice, complimented her on how pretty Edna looked, and how well all their daughters' weddings had been organised.

'Only our Ivy to be married now,' said Alice, 'and she's courting. Ron works at the aircraft factory too.'

'That's good,' replied Harriet, 'then if there is a war, he won't be called up.'

'Oh Harriet, there's not going to be a war!' exclaimed Alice. 'Don't even think about it.'

'Well, not today,' said Harriet and took her place in the photo lineup.

Edna and Len intended to start their married life in rented rooms for a year or two, as did most young married couples. Harriet suggested they could live with her and Fred; they could have the downstairs back room as their living room, leaving Harriet and Fred the front parlour and the breakfast room. The front bedroom was now empty as the lodgers had left: Charlie had moved to another town and Lawrence had a new job the other side of the city. He promised to keep in touch and visit them all from time to time.

As events transpired, Edna and Len lived with Harriet far longer than two years.

Chapter 8

WAR AGAIN

HARRIET, FRED, Len and Edna clustered around the radio, Edna nursing baby Sheila, as they listened to the Prime Minister's announcement, that he had declared war on Germany. Chamberlain had abandoned his policy of appeasement by March 1939 when Germany embarked on further aggressions in Czechoslovakia; Britain then pledged support to Poland, Greece, Rumania and Turkey. When Poland was invaded, Britain issued an ultimatum to Germany to withdraw; this was ignored, so Britain declared war in September. Commonwealth countries pledged to support Britain.

Fred was pale. 'I never thought I'd live to see the day again,' he said quietly.

'No, I'm sure you didn't,' Len affirmed, 'but I think Germany has been preparing for this for some time. I'm not sure how well prepared we are though. I'm sure we shall be very busy at the B.A.C. from now on.'

'Well at least you will be more use to the country here than going off fighting somewhere,' said Harriet, 'and you're too old this time, Fred. I don't know about Reg or Tom.'

It transpired that Reg had a congenital chest condition which exempted him from active service, and Tom, working for Cowlin's, one of the major building companies, was deemed to be more use at home than at the front, although he was later transferred to the engineering workshops at Patchway.

Preparations for war began immediately, the British

HARRIET'S FAMILY

Expeditionary Force were sent to France in the second week of September, to meet up with French forces defending the Belgian border. At home the blackout was instigated as a precaution against air attacks, people were issued with ration books for food, clothing and household goods, although these were not utilised immediately. Everyone was given a gas mask, which they were instructed to carry at all times. Infants under one year, which included Sheila, were issued with a chamber which looked like a small carry-cot with a transparent face cover, in which the baby had to be completely enclosed.

Edna's stomach turned over as she looked at it. 'I do hope I never have to use this, it looks horrendous.' Her own claustrophobia was surfacing.

The garden at the back of the house was too small to accomodate an Anderson shelter. Alice and Reg had one installed in their garden so it was planned that any of Harriet's household could also use it during air raids. However it would have taken at least five minutes to leave Harriet's house and run to Alice's air raid shelter, by which time the bombs would be dropping, so they only used it a few times. At other times they simply sheltered under the kitchen table, a substantial item made by Fred. When baby Sheila entered her second year she was issued with a Mickey Mouse gas mask, which fortunately she never had to wear although Edna viewed it with less trepidation than the cot.

They listened to the news, but neither the Germans nor the Allied Forces took any major initiatives in the first few months of the war, although the German U-boats harried the Royal Navy and Merchant Navy. British children who had been evacuated to the countryside in October and November began to return to their homes. Then, without warning, Germany invaded Denmark, Norway and the Low Countries during the first half of 1940. From here the subsequent attack on France drove the Allied Forces back to the French coast. Chamberlain resigned as Prime Minister and Winston Churchill took his place as leader. British and French troops evacuated from Dunkirk in June in a flotilla of small boats, as there were not enough troopships to carry them.

'Shows a lack of organisation,' said Harriet. 'Muddling through as usual. What would they have done, without those fishermen and other sailors coming to the rescue?'

'Seems like nothing has changed in twenty-odd years,' replied Fred. 'I bet they had to leave most of the equipment on the beaches too. When I was in France, each time we had to retreat they left machine guns and equipment behind. Now they are saying Petain has asked Hitler for an armistice for France; a lot of the French won't like that, to them, Germany is still the old enemy.'

The following week Lilian and Joyce called to visit Harriet. 'Did you see it in the paper, some of the men who came back from Dunkirk are arriving in Bristol today and will be billeted in those Nissan huts at the top of Eastville Park.'

'No I didn't see that in the paper,' Harriet replied, 'but I did wonder what those new huts would be used for. I noticed them the other day, when I cut through the park from Fishponds Road.'

'Joyce and I are going to see them arrive and give them a cheer,' Lilian said. 'Do you want to come with us?'

'No, the baby's only just gone off to sleep, and Edna's gone out to get some shopping. But you go, the poor souls could do with a welcome. What a nightmare that must have been for them.'

Lil and Joyce set off through the park, to Fishponds Road entrance. Once again much of the grass had been removed so that allotments could be planted. The railings and huge gates had been removed, as the metal was needed for the war effort; this prefaced the removal of railings from domestic and commercial properties. There was a small crowd waiting at the denuded entrance to the park, and Lil and Joyce joined them. Shortly afterwards lorries began arriving and men in khaki uniforms alighted, some wearing bandages, some needing assistance from their comrades. Most glanced quizzically at the waiting crowd, who began to cheer and wave to them. Grins appeared on their drawn faces and they waved back, before entering the Nissan huts, which would be their homes during recuperation.

Until that time the war had been a remote reality. There had been few bombing raids on Britain, but in July Germany began her attack to disable the planes of the Royal Air Force prior to a planned invasion by sea in September; the battle for Britain had commenced.

One of the first daylight raids in Bristol attacked the Filton aircraft works, on September 25th. Len, fortunately, had managed to arrange to have the day off, as it was Edna's birthday. They had left Harriet looking after Sheila while they went into town, to buy Edna's birthday present, when they saw the planes pass over; Len knew at once they were German. With that the air raid warnings sounded.

'They look to be heading for Filton, we'd better go straight home,' he told Edna. They were worried because Eastville was only a few miles from Filton.

Harriet too saw the planes coming over and heard the sirens. She was in the garden, hanging out washing, and immediately ran indoors, grabbed seventeen-month old Sheila and both crouched under the table until the all-clear sounded.

The planes dropped 100 tons of bombs in fifteen seconds; sixty people were killed when the factory air raid shelters were hit, a further thirty employees were killed and two hundred injured. The Rodney Works and the Gipsy Patch Lane workshops were extensively damaged, while a stray stick of bombs hit an unfinished housing estate at Filton, fortunately unoccupied.

Viewed as a success by the Luftwaffe, a similar attack was launched two days late, but foiled by a squadron of Hurricanes now posted at Filton. There was no damage or loss of life on this occasion. These two conflicts were subsequently recognised as among the last few of the Battle of Britain. Britain's secret radar system indicated to the Royal Air Force where the enemy planes were, and the Battle of Britain raged on into September, until Hitler was forced to abandon his plans to invade the country as Germany had lost so many aircraft.

'Never in the field of human conflict was so much owed by so many to so few,' was Churchill's tribute to the Air Force in one of his speeches to the nation. He was a great communicator, although Harriet and Fred were both sure that the nation was only being told what was good for them, just as had occurred in the Great War.

Air attacks on Britain continued fairly regularly, mainly at night although there were still a few daylight raids. Bristol was often a target, being a large conurbation and having an aircraft factory.

Harriet had walked to the nearby shops at Eastville centre, when the air raid warning began. Shops emptied and shoppers and passers-by ran for the public air raid shelter there, near the Black Swan public house. Harriet hesitated for a few seconds, but realised she would have to use the public shelter, as it would take her at least ten minutes to reach home. When the 'all-clear' sounded she emerged and was too shaken and upset to finish her shopping, and hurried directly home. An Air Raid Warden had told the people emerging from the shelter that the planes had passed over and no bombs dropped locally, but she was still concerned for Edna and the baby at home.

Subsequent to this experience Edna decided that when she went shopping in town, she would leave her daughter with Harriet. One Saturday shopping trip in November Edna had made all her planned purchases, when she saw a pair of vases which she fell in love with. On her return home she told Harriet.

'If you really like them, I'll buy you them for you and Len for Christmas,' said Harriet. 'But you'd better go back and buy them on Monday or they will be gone.'

But 'gone' they were by Monday. During Sunday night, 24th November 1940, a bombing raid demolished the entire shopping area around Castle Street. Nothing remained of Bristol's central shops or a number of Bristol's historic buildings, including the exquisite 17th century Dutch House.

That Sunday afternoon Lilian, Tom and Joyce had been visiting Harriet and the family at Heath Road, as was their custom on a weekend. They stayed to tea and were preparing to leave about eight-thirty in the evening when the air raid siren sounded. They stood at Harriet's front door, deciding whether to continue on homeward. Tom had to leave as he was on Home Guard duty, as were Len and Fred, but he urged Lilian and Joyce to stay with Harriet. Later that night, Harriet, Lilian and Edna watched the red glow in the night sky as central Bristol, five miles away, burned.

Reg, Alice's husband, had not joined the Home Guard but was an Air Raid Warden. Many evenings he was on patrol, fire-watching and ensuring that no lights were shown at house or shop windows. The black-out had to be complete so as to not give enemy aircraft clues as to conurbations or factories. The morning after the blitz, still wearing his Air Raid Warden's uniform, Reg came to see that they were all well. Alice and Ken had spent the night in the air raid shelter, he said, and central Bristol is devastated. 'Completely flattened, we've been told. No shops left. Some of Bedminster took a hammering too. Fortunately there was no damage in St Werburgh's, so Lil has a house to go home to.'

A few days later Harriet put on her hat and coat and went to see what had happened to her beloved city. She was aghast.

'All those buildings were there before I was born, and now they're all gone. Even the churches are damaged, St. Nicks, St Mary-le-Port—St Peter's is just a shell.'

The local newspapers carried reports of bomb damage extending to Bedminster and there were photographs of homes reduced to rubble. Harriet was concerned, as it was her old home district and she still had relations who lived there. She continued her tour of investigation.

Cabot Street where the family shop had been located was totally destroyed, as were many of the neighbouring streets. The section of Whitehouse Lane where Harriet's family had lived was also flattened; fortunately Harriet's sister and her family had moved to Knowle a few years before the war.

Harriet stood by the ruins of St John's Church; she had attended Sunday School there as a child. She thought about her wedding to

Bill Fricker, which had taken place there, and all the other family weddings and christenings. Although they had not been great church-goers, the Bolts always thought of it as their church. Like St Peter's, only a shell of a building remained. The Bedminster of Harriet's childhood was gone. She stood for some time in the ruined churchyard, feeling as though all the air had been sucked from her lungs, all the substance from her body. Then with some trepidation she rounded the corner into Phillip Street where George Henry and Teresa still lived. She breathed a sigh of relief; the houses were untouched at that end of the road. She knocked at the door, suddenly desperate to see them.

Teresa welcomed her with open arms.

'Oh God it was so frightening, Harriet, I've never been so frightened in all my life. It was so close. We heard the sirens and I went down the air raid shelter at the end of the road, George put on his helmet and gas mask and went to the Warden's point. When I came out again everything was in ruins and there were fires everywhere. The brigade was using hoses, so there was water running down the gutters as well. I didn't know where George was or even if he was alive; I didn't know if our house was still standing. First of all we weren't allowed up this road till they were sure it was safe, then I found the house was all right, and our George came back an hour or so later, black as soot and very tired, but at least he was safe. They had pulled so many people out of bombed houses during the night, some dead, some alive. You feel so helpless when you are bombed in your own home; there's nowhere to run to, nowhere is safe any more. You always expect your home to be a sanctuary, but not nowadays.'

'Well thank goodness you're both safe,' said Harriet. 'How about young George?' She was referring to Teresa's son.

'Oh, he and his wife and the baby are safe,' Teresa replied. 'He wasn't eligible for the last call-up, as he's over thirty, but he may have to go next time.'

Harriet thought to herself, this is a good time not to have sons. She remembered how her mother had spent the years of the Great

War worrying, and had lost two of her three sons. She walked back through the ruins of Bedminster to her bus stop. When she reached home she told Edna what Teresa had said, that there was nowhere to run to now they were being attacked in their own homes.

'That's the difference between this war and the last,' she said. 'Then soldiers went to the Front to fight, now we are all in it, whether we like it or not. I wonder if Churchill realised it would be like this? Surely somebody did.'

'You feel so powerless, you can't even protect your children,' said Edna, glancing at her daughter.

'I feel so sorry for those poor souls whose homes have been totally destroyed, they have nothing and nowhere to go unless relatives take them in. I know they are supposed to get compensation, but that's not what matters,' mused Harriet. 'If your home's gone that's your security gone.'

It seemed that most air raids occurred when both Fred and Len were not at home. Their respective workplaces had instigated round-the-clock shifts to maximise production. Both Harriet and Edna preferred to risk staying in the house, crouching under the stairs or under the dining table, rather than running to Alice's shelter. At the first warning, Edna would take Sheila from her cot, wrap them both in her winter coat and settle on the pile of quilts under the table, where Harriet would join her. Evenings at home were rare for Fred and Len even when they were not at work, as both had joined the Home Guard, although Len said it was a complete waste of time. There were no uniforms or weapons; they drilled using broomsticks instead of rifles.

'If we are invaded I shall have to hit the enemy over the head with my broomstick before he shoots me,' he told Edna dryly.

'Well, Tom seems to think his Home Guard duties are necessary,' she replied.

'Yes, but his father's a policeman, so maybe he's used to the idea of following orders.' Len had an independent streak and did not take kindly to authoritarian attitudes when he could not see the sense or the value of them. He never accepted rules at face-value, but always questioned the reasons for them. He was a staunch Union supporter, although there was little Union activity during wartime. He hated the night-shift at Filton. 'There are so many air raid warnings we spend most of the night in the shelters,' he told Edna. 'You can't get much work done. And they are so damp; some of them have a couple of inches of water in them.'

The following year, on the night of 16th March 1941, the air raid sirens sounded, followed by the hum of aircraft engines over east Bristol then the whine and explosion of bombs, louder and closer than ever before. Fred and Len were both at work; Edna and Harriet had followed their usual routine and were downstairs with Sheila, who was almost two years old by this time. The child was wide-eyed but quiet, used to the disrupted nights, but clutching at her mother at each new, loud noise.

Harriet looked at Sheila. Poor little soul, she thought, all she's known all her young life is war, bombs and disturbed nights. No sweets, few toys. What are we doing to these children? Aloud she said,

'This is closer than it's ever been before, Edna. I wonder what we'd better do.' Both women were frightened.

'I think it's probably too dangerous now to go to the shelter,' Edna replied. 'Shall we look outside and see?'

They turned off the hall light to comply with the blackout and opened the front door, Edna holding her daughter in her arms. The sky to the west glowed brilliant red, orange where it silhouetted the railway arches and houses on Muller Road, graduating to a darker red as it faded upwards into the night sky. There was a dull roaring sound, a backdrop to the sirens, explosions and anti-aircraft guns. As they looked out, half a dozen men wearing tin helmets came running along the road towards the source of the glow. They were the Air Raid Wardens; one of them was Reg, Alice's husband. Harriet called out to him and he stopped at the gate.

'Whatever is it, Reg?'

'Don't worry, Ma, it's only the Gas Works gone up. We are going there now, go back inside and shut the door,' he called.

Harriet went cold, she slumped back against the doorframe, was she to lose another husband to a violent death?

'Oh my God, Reg, do hurry. Father is over there, he's on nights this week.'

'All right, Ma, but do go inside and shut the door, you are showing a light.' Reg ran on; they were not really showing a light but he didn't want them to stand in the doorway watching and waiting.

They went into the breakfast room and Harriet sat down, before her legs turned to jelly. Edna placed Sheila on Harriet's lap while she went to make a pot of tea. There were no further thoughts of running to the shelter; later they lay, sleepless, under the table, listening. Several times they peered through the blackout curtains, watching shadowy figures running along the street, with the blood-red sky as a backdrop. The bombing that night raged on for eight hours altogether.

Dawn had broken when they heard a key turn in the lock; Fred had returned home. At last his wife and daughter could release the pent-up tears, now tears of relief. Fred recounted his experiences, as Sheila slept on, under the table.

'The warning siren sounded, and my mate and I dashed for the air raid shelter. He got to the workshop door before me and grabbed the door handle, when the door blew off in his hand. The blast knocked us both through the door, we landed in a heap— him still clutching the door handle! The building behind us was on fire so we ran for the air raid shelter at the far end of the site. It was all mayhem after that; every time we tried to come out we were sent back as there were still bombs falling. They must have bombed all of Easton as well.'

'I do hope our Lil and Joyce are safe, they would be next in line at St Werburghs,' said Harriet. 'When you go up to bed, I'll go round there and see they are all right.'

Lilian and Joyce were safe having spent the night under the stairs, except for a few minutes spent gazing with fascination at the flames roaring out of the gasometer at the top of the road and the red glow in the sky all around. Tom had been at work, and returned to his home with great trepidation. He was relieved to find his family safe, the only problem being that all the windows had been blown out, as had most of the other houses in the street, but he felt that was a small price to pay. He changed into his Home Guard uniform and went on duty for several hours, before snatching two hours sleep, then returning to work for the next night shift. By the time he returned home the following morning, he was so tired he fell into bed and slept soundly until Lil roused him for work again. He had not even stirred when the workmen came and replaced all the windows, even in the bedroom where he was sleeping!

Harriet was thankful that her family was unharmed by the closest air raid yet, but grieved for the two hundred and fifty-seven people who were killed and the four hundred injured. As well as destroying homes, St Barnabas Church had taken a direct hit, twenty-four people who were taking sanctuary there were killed and many others injured. German records later showed that 162 aircraft had dropped 166 tons of high explosive bombs and 940 incendiary containers during that raid. Only one man was killed at the Gas Works, Mr Morgan, a firewatcher.

Churchill visited Bristol one month later, to view the damage and promote the war-spirit; there was another blitz the night he arrived, targeting the Park Street area. On his tour next day he received a mixed reception from the people of Bristol, some waved and cheered, others, who blamed him and the government for their plight, booed as he passed.

There were air defences near Eastville; sited on Purdown Hill, between Eastville and Filton was a large anti-aircraft gun, which the locals nicknamed 'Purdown Percy' which made enough noise to terrify the residents and may have been a deterrent for enemy aircraft, though it scored few hits. There were also two air balloons, tethered by strong cables, one at Purdown, another in Eastville Park.

Harriet was sitting in the garden one afternoon with Edna and Lilian and their two children when they saw one of the air balloons wobbling loose in the sky. It seemed to be heading directly towards them and they ran indoors, but at the last moment it veered and landed on the roof of the house next door, bursting into flames. Edna was on her way to call the elderly lady who lived there when she appeared in the garden, safe but understandably very upset. The Fire Brigade promptly appeared, having been alerted when the balloon first broke its moorings, and they soon had the blaze under control; the drama was enhanced when one of the firemen put his foot through the roof and had to be rescued.

The aircraft and engineering works at Filton and Patchway, north of Bristol, would have been prime targets and had to be camouflaged; false runways with lights were laid on top of the Mendips, south of Bristol, to decoy German bombs aimed for Filton. Yet it was the unfinished airport at Lulsgate, later to become Bristol Airport, which actually captured a German plane. The plane had lost its navigational aids and landed, thinking it was in France, right into the arms of bemused builders and security patrols.

Edna and her friend Vera decided they should do something to help the war effort. While Harriet looked after Sheila, the two young women enrolled in Red Cross evening classes for First Aid.

Edna loved it; this was what she wanted to do. When her final results came through at the end of the course she had achieved 98%. She was called to receive congratulations from the Head of the Red Cross in the Bristol area, who told her that no-one had ever before achieved such a high mark. Edna, flushed with success, enrolled in the next course, which was Child Welfare. Vera's baby was due and she was unable to enroll at that time.

Successfully completing her second course, Edna wondered

about nursing. She discussed it with Len and Harriet, who both encouraged her; Harriet offered to look after Sheila when neither of her parents was available. Edna wrote her letter of application, which Len adjusted, and Edna was offered a post as a student nurse at the Bristol Royal Infirmary.

'It won't be much money during the three years I'm a student,' she told Len, 'but I'm sure I can save some and after the war we should have enough money for a house of our own.'

Edna thoroughly enjoyed nursing, it was what she had always wanted. She found the B.R.I. a very formal establishment, she told Harriet. 'I was going to lunch at the same time as our Staff Nurse; she and I get on well together. As we went in the dining room the supervisor there told us to sit in separate sections, because she was trained staff and I wasn't. Even when she asked if I could sit with her, the woman just said, you know the rules.'

On another occasion Edna was going off duty, crossing the yard outside the wards with her nursing cap in her hand, when she was stopped by a Sister.

'Put your cap on, please, nurse.'

'I have lost one of my white hairgrips, Sister' replied Edna, 'but I am off duty now.'

'That doesn't matter, nurse, you are in uniform. Fix your cap as best you can with one grip,' was the reply.

In other ways the formal regime worked in Edna's favour. While working on the children's ward, Edna was airing a child's rubber sheet on the balcony rail; when she went to retrieve it she found it had slipped and fallen to the ground several floors below. On offering to fetch it she was told to simply ring for a porter who would return it to the ward. There were also ward maids at the hospital, there were no nursing staff cleaning and polishing floors as in many other hospitals, nurses there were nurses.

Harriet, meanwhile, was holding the home together. She was doing the housework, washing, cooking meals for four adults and looking after a two-year-old. She was fifty-five years old by this time and found it harder than she had expected to do all she deemed necessary. She did the baby's washing and many other tasks so that Edna would not have too much to do when she returned from work. Mealtimes were not easy; Fred, Len and Edna were all working shifts, and it was very rare that shifts coincided or people arrived home for meals at the same time. Harriet felt that she was working harder than ever before, but did not complain, she was doing her duty. Alice, living close by, would often fetch Harriet's shopping with her own. Lilian was a great help; her daughter, Joyce, was at school during the day, so she would visit Harriet and often take Sheila home with her, returning when Joyce came home from school. The two cousins formed a strong bond, almost like sisters. Harriet was glad of this; she was very concerned that Sheila's solitary games with her dolls and Teddy consisted of hiding under the table and pretending they had been bombed out of their home. She needs other children, thought Harriet.

Rationing had not made housekeeping an easy task; it took all Harriet's ingenuity to produce the type of meals she felt was acceptable. For the past ten years she had shopped at the local shops; the shop owners all knew her and often saved her choice items which were only rarely available. Dried egg was fine in cakes, Harriet thought, but you need fresh eggs for omelettes, contrary to the publicity. Fortunately Alice and Reg had a back garden large enough for a chicken-run, and during the summer months had surplus eggs. Some of the kitchen scraps were saved for the chickens, others went into the pig-bins issued by the local authority. These were collected regularly and the contents boiled for pig-feed. Even the tea-leaves were not thrown away, but carefully tipped onto the garden, as Fred said they were good for the roses.

Eastville Park's allotments had been offered to local residents, but Harriet's family decided they did not have time to take on any further commitments. Fred grew runner beans and a few salad vegetables in their tiny back garden. Somehow they managed well, Harriet thought, but it was a hand-to-mouth existence.

Fred's eldest brother, Uriah or Yewey as everyone now called him, had retired from work a few years previously and rented a large piece of land at Frenchay, which he had developed as a market garden. His wife had died some years previously; he ostensibly lived with his son at Frenchay, but felt that his son's wife did not welcome him there, so he had a bed in the back of his market garden shed which was where he spent his summer nights. He owned a pony and cart, and drove from Frenchay to Eastville delivering the vegetables he had grown, always keeping the best for Harriet's family, and making her his last call before returning home to his market garden. He always came into the house for a cup of tea and piece of homemade cake, or sometimes a meal; Tony the pony munched his way through his nosebag of feed while he waited, usually attended by Sheila, whose great love of horses stemmed from that time. Sometimes Uncle Yewey let her drive the pony and cart to the end of the road, once she was old enough to run back home on her own, Harriet watching anxiously from the gate.

There was no fuel for private transport; businesses which had never progressed beyond horse and cart transport now found they were in vogue again. The milkman, who was always the owner of his small-business, delivered each day from a horse and cart. Mr Culliford delivered milk to Harriet's family; milk from the churns on the cart was dipped out with a measuring jug into one of Harriet's clean white china jugs. It was covered with a muslin cloth and placed in the wire mesh fronted safe, in a shady part of the back garden. Milkmen usually had white horses and coalmen had black horses; Harriet's tradesmen were no exception. She knew all of them by name and always asked after their families.

Ellen called to see Harriet one afternoon. When they were settled with a cup of tea, and Sheila was sitting on the rug eating the apple Ellen had brought her, Ellen said,

'Harriet, I'm thinking of getting married again.'

'Are you?' Harriet could not conceal her surprise, after all Ellen was past sixty.

'His name is Bill Howe, he's a widower, ten years older than me. He's a nice man, very kind and thoughtful; you'd like him, Harriet. We have a great deal in common, and he needs someone to look after him and I think I would like to do that.'

Ellen told Harriet that she had attended a social gathering with George and Saranne and began talking to a man who said he had lived most of his life near Timsbury and intended to return there after the war, he was only living in Bristol to help with the war-effort. As Ellen had been born at Timsbury, the two found they had a great deal to talk about. They had met a number of times since and on the last occasion Bill had proposed marriage, and suggested they should both return to Timsbury at the end of the war.

'I've been to see Amy, to talk it over with her. She thinks it's a good idea, if I feel I can be happy with him,' Ellen said, 'then I thought I'd come and see you next.'

Harriet was delighted for her friend, and offered her home for the wedding breakfast. They stretched the rations somehow, and Edna prepared the celebratory meal while Harriet and Amy attended the wedding ceremony. Bill and Ellen visited Bill's cottage at Bloomfield, just outside of Timsbury, although it had been rented to a family for the duration of the war.

The war dragged on; there were fewer air raids after mid-1941, but life did not seem any easier. Living at that level of stress took its toll on most people and Harriet's family was no exception. Constant shift work was tiring and tempers frayed. Len had difficulty sleeping during the day, and when Edna returned from the hospital he often complained he had not been able to sleep because their daughter was making a noise and crying.

'I don't know if your mother's looking after her properly, why doesn't she take her out more often?' he grumbled querulously.

'If she was out all the time you'd have a dirty house and no hot meals,' Edna retorted, but the grumbling was upsetting her.

Eventually, early in 1943 she gave in her notice at the hospital; she had completed more than half of her nursing training. Matron was furious.

'We would never have taken you on if we had thought you wouldn't finish the course,' she said angrily. 'There's all that training wasted. Someone else could have had your place.'

Edna was upset, but felt there was nothing else she could do. When she returned home and told Len he felt guilty and told her there was no need for her to give up the work she loved.

'Too late now,' said Edna. 'I am working a month's notice. Now perhaps we can all get some peace.'

Peace was still far off, but life became less fraught for those at home when the air raids ceased and the war news was encouraging. Germany had unsuccessfully invaded Russian territory, which made the Russians take an active role against the Germans, and when the Japanese bombed American ships at Pearl Harbour the Americans also joined the Allies. When Italy capitulated to invading Allied troops in 1943 Germany was fighting alone in Europe with Japan waging war in the east. Yet somehow the war churned on. They kept abreast of the news by listening to the radio; patriotism was promoted visually by the Pathe News items included at the cinema. Both Harriet and Edna loved films, and one or other of them often took Sheila with them to His Majesty's cinema at Eastville from an early age. The child was fascinated by the images on the screen and sat quietly watching, whether she understood or not. Walking home from the cinema Harriet would explain items from the Pathe News or the film to her grand-daughter, and often fill in background information not always made available on screen.

As a gesture towards normality Harriet suggested that she and Edna should take Sheila on a week's holiday to Weston-super-Mare. Harriet loved the coast and was missing the seaside holidays they used to take. Len and Fred were busy at work, so the two women set off by train, having found lodgings in the centre of the town. Unfortunately the weather was not kind to them, it was too windy to sit on the beach and they seemed to have chosen a week when the tide was out every day, so there was no paddling for Harriet and Sheila. Sheila was very upset, she thought that they should have spent every day on the beach, windy or not, and found no consolation looking round the town shops, most of which were unscathed by the blitz. They returned at the end of their week not feeling refreshed. Ah well, thought Harriet, I tried.

Sheila started school in 1944; she found that she was one of the few children in the class to still have a father living at home. She came home from school for lunch on her first day, having spent the morning threading coloured beads on a string which then had to be unthreaded and put back in the box, so she felt she had spent a futile morning. Fred, who had also arrived home for lunch, asked how she had enjoyed school.

'Not very much,' she replied. 'We didn't learn anything, they haven't taught me to read or write yet. I don't think I'll bother to go any more, it's a waste of time.'

Fred laughed heartily. 'You can't pick and choose,' he said, 'Once you've started you have to keep going.' He was very fond of his grand-daughter; she shared his interest in gardening and knew the names of most of the flowers in the garden. He was never impatient or cross, always gentle and kind and would go to great lengths to explain simply how different types of plants required different treatments. She had a patch of garden of her own, which she tended carefully, and Fred had just taught her to disbud chrysanthemums. What was more, she liked eating the snails Fred cooked. He tugged her plaits and went indoors for his lunch. He knew that Sheila would follow him in and sit by his side while he ate, accepting choice morsels from his plate.

'Fred, she's had her lunch,' Harriet would say, but Fred would only smile.

'It tastes better off my plate, doesn't it?'

In February 1945 Edna and Len had another daughter, Patricia.

They had intended to wait until the end of the war to increase their family, but the war was taking so long, the gap between their two children would soon mean there would be little rapport between the siblings. Even so, Sheila was a little disappointed that her new sister was unable to come out in the street to play, a new milestone that she herself had only just passed.

At last the war was over; victory was marked by numerous street parties and celebrations. Troops returned home, Air Force squadrons returned; Sheila and Harriet stood at the front gate one day and counted a formation of over one hundred aircraft heading north-east. Harriet thought to herself, nice not to have to feel we must run indoors. American GIs in England were gradually being repatriated. Edna and Len were returning from the park one day, when they met three Americans in uniform walking towards them, who asked if the little girl would like some gum. Naturally Sheila said yes please, she had heard about gum although she had never tried any. After they walked on she glanced back at them, puzzled.

'What is it?' asked Edna, but Sheila could not express what she wanted to say.

'That man –' she tried, but shook her head.

'Did you notice his skin was black?' asked Edna.

'Yes,' said Sheila, 'why was that?'

'Because he probably came from Africa originally,' her father explained. 'It's a very hot country and having a black skin gives protection against the sun. That's the only difference.' Sheila was satisfied with this explanation; it was the first black person she had ever seen as there were virtually none in Bristol at that time.

Life gradually returned to something akin to its prewar norm. Tom returned to work at Cowlins, Reg to Cashmore's new premises, as the old building had been destroyed in the blitz, Len and Fred no longer had to work night shifts. Edna busied herself with her new baby and Sheila settled into school, finding it more interesting as time progressed. Having spent her formative years with adults she showed a grown-up type of reasoning. Shortly after the war they received a mailshot promoting Tate and Lyle sugar; there was a cutout page which could be made into a comic 'Mr Cube' with slot-in feet to make him stand up. Sheila put together Mr Cube and then pointed out to her father the significance of the slogan on the base.

'Look, it says, *I stand on my own feet*. That's clever, because you can also take it that he doesn't want to be nationalised.'

Len was astounded; he looked at Edna and Harriet, who shook their heads, then back at Sheila. 'How do you know about nationalising sugar?' he asked. No one at home had discussed it and he didn't think it was taught to seven-year-olds at school.

'It was on the news, on the radio the other day. There's lots of things they're thinking of nationalising and sugar was one of them.'

Harriet frowned; what sort of world was this where little children kept apace of the political situation? The family's preoccupation with listening to the news on the radio had been passed on to the child. Then she smiled and looked around her at her family; they had come through unscathed, unlike her mother's experiences of war.

Chapter 9

A DEPARTURE AND MANY NEW ARRIVALS

During the school summer holidays Harriet took Ken, Joyce and Sheila to visit Ellen, now living in Bill's cottage at Bloomfield, a tiny village near Timsbury; Bill owned one of a terrace of cottages along a track from the main road. While Harriet chatted to Ellen, the three children had a wonderful time wandering freely across the fields which smelled of new-mown hay. After a good lunch Ellen took Harriet and the children to visit her brother Sam, who was farming not more than a mile or so from where she now lived.

It was a hot day, and the mile seemed long, through dusty country lanes, but no one grumbled. Sheila thought it seemed like an adventure out of one of her Enid Blyton books. The inside of the farmhouse was cool and dark; Sam's wife gave them tea and lemonade, and called Sam in from the cowhouse to talk to them.

He talked about his animals and his acreage.

'I've got the five acre field down to corn this year,' he said, 'we've had the cows in on it once.'

'Oh that's a shame, Sam,' said Harriet, who really knew nothing about farming.

'No, no,' said Sam, 'that's what you do. You get the cows in on the new corn and they nibble down the shoots, then that grows again, so you get two shoots instead of one.'

Later that afternoon they walked back to Ellen's cottage. Ellen's husband, Bill, had returned from the visit he had been making during the day; he solemnly shook hands with each of the children and walked with them to the bus stop. Sheila told her grandmother how much she had enjoyed the day. Ellen had invited Harriet for a week's stay and Harriet promised she would write and ask if Sheila might accompany her.

They set off two weeks later for five days stay with Ellen and Bill. When they alighted from the bus at the stop near the Bloomfield public house, they were a few elderly men sitting at a table outside together with a man who was bent almost double, leaning on a pair of crutches. Harriet nodded and walked down the lane to Ellen's cottage. When the preliminary greetings were made, Harriet asked Ellen about the man with crutches.

'Yes, that's old Albert, he was tossed by a bull when he was a young man. It broke his back and that's how it set. He manages to get about on his crutches, but he's never been able to work since.'

Sheila's eyes were round, so Harriet added, for her benefit, 'If you see a bull in the field, don't go in!'

'They're usually fine if they've got the cows with them,' said Ellen.

'Well I wouldn't risk it anyway,' said Harriet and her granddaughter silently agreed.

'So I suppose,' Ellen continued, 'when he dies, they will have to break his back again to get him into the coffin.'

'Not much else they could do,' agreed Harriet. Sheila did not like the turn of the conversation and wandered out into the front garden; old people were always talking about death. As she returned to the front door a few minutes later she heard Aunt Ellen say,

'He will keep calling me Mary, of course that was his first wife's name. It's usually if he's dropped off to sleep in his chair and wakes up with a start, then I'm always Mary. I get so sick of it. One day I shouted at him, I'll give you Mary!'

And she demonstrated, singing one of the popular songs of the day, marching up and down in the tiny room,

*'Mary, Mary, long before the fashions changed
And there is something rare
It sounds so square
It's a grand old name.'*

'Ellen, you didn't!' exclaimed Harriet.
The two women suddenly caught sight of the little girl in the doorway, her mouth open wide, and both burst out laughing. Relieved, the child laughed too.
'You must think I'm a funny old auntie,' said Ellen. 'Come in now, and have a drink and a piece of cake.'
Later Harriet said to Ellen, 'You'll have to forgive Bill, Ellen, remember he is quite a bit older than you, his brain doesn't work as fast as yours, especially if he's been asleep, he takes longer to wake up.'
'Well I suppose so,' grumbled Ellen, 'but it is irritating.'

The cottage was in a row of similar two-up two-down dwellings, with a long garden at the front, where flowers bordered the path and vegetables grew behind the flowers. At the back of the cottage was a small cobbled yard, with an outside privy. Behind the high wall cows mooed and entranced the child, at a safe distance.
The front door of the cottage opened directly into the living room. On the left was the kitchen range, where Ellen cooked huge country meals and always kept a kettle boiling. By the side of the range was Bill's easy chair, where he dozed after meals—and at other times during the day. On the right of the room was a large, old leather sofa, where Harriet and Sheila sat for their meals, Sheila on two cushions; the kitchen table was drawn up to the sofa, Ellen and Bill sat on Windsor chairs on the other side.
A door in the corner of the room concealed the stairs, with their sharp turn; the top of the stairs led directly into the room shared by Harriet and Sheila. The main piece of furniture was a

large bed with a feather mattress, so comfortable that the child could not fail but go to sleep, however hard she tried to stay awake and watch the night darkening over the cows in the field behind the cottage. She usually managed to stay awake until her grandmother came to bed and was greatly amused to hear Harriet say, every night, 'Oh, it's so lovely to have a bed to go to. Pity some poor folks who've got no bed.'

'Oh surely that's not right, Gran,' said Sheila, giggling. 'Everyone's got a bed, especially now the war's over. We've all got beds and houses.'

'Don't you be so sure,' Harriet replied, but the child remained unconvinced. Where did one find these people with no beds?

During the week Sheila met one of the neighbour's children, May, and the two girls played together, while Harriet and Ellen spent most of the week talking. One afternoon they all walked into Timsbury; Sheila was amazed that these country people thought nothing of walking miles; at home you went by bus. But when their stay had come to an end she was genuinely sorry to leave, as was Harriet.

'I wouldn't mind living out here,' she told Ellen. 'Perhaps when Fred retires, he's only got another four years at work. He's due to retire in nineteen fifty.'

'It would be nice to have you as a neighbour,' said Ellen wistfully; she had enjoyed Harriet's company. But it was not to be.

Harriet was concerned about Fred; she had commented on his cough after he returned from the war in 1919 when he had blamed the gas in the trenches; she had blamed the Woodbines he smoked constantly. As a concession to her ten or eleven years ago he had stopped smoking cigarettes and taken up a pipe. But recently his cough seemed worse. Harriet tried to persuade him to see their doctor, but Fred refused.

'There's nothing wrong with me, it's just a bit of a cough. He can't undo what was done in the War,' he said, and went out into his beloved garden to preclude further argument.

When Harriet next went to the doctor's for a check-up, she mentioned Fred's cough. She had developed a slightly irregular heartbeat possibly as a result of the rheumatic fever she had as a young woman, and had to take digitalis, which was monitored from time to time. Thanks to the newly-introduced Health Service she no longer had to pay for doctor's visits or tablets.

'How long has he had this cough?' asked Dr Purcell.

'Since before 1918, doctor, but it has got much worse in the past six months.'

Dr Purcell thought carefully; Fred never came to the surgery, he hadn't seen him as a patient for years; the last time he saw him in passing was when Edna's youngest child was born two years ago.

'Will he be home on Saturday afternoon? If so I will call in, I will say it's to see you about your tablets, and I'll comment on his cough and insist on listening to his chest.'

On Saturday afternoon Dr Purcell's Riley RME drew up outside Harriet's house. Fred and Sheila were in the front garden tending the flowers.

'Hello doctor, didn't expect to see you,' said Fred, opening the gate.

'I wanted to check that Harriet is all right on her new tablets,' said the doctor. 'Is she in, Fred?'

'Yes, follow me, doctor,' Fred dutifully led the way, coughing as he went.

Sheila stayed in the garden, gazing at the car; she thought it was the most beautiful car she had ever seen, green with a black fabric covered roof. One day I'll have a car like that, she vowed. The only other person she knew who owned a car was Mr Marsh, who lived two doors away, he owned a garage so was expected to have a car, but it wasn't as nice as this one.

In the breakfastroom Dr Purcell had asked Harriet if her tablets suited her, then turned to Fred immediately, before he could escape to the garden again.

'I don't like the sound of that cough, Fred. Let me listen to your chest, maybe I could give you some cough medicine for it.'

Fred submitted to the examination, at the end of which Jack Purcell's face looked grave.

'I don't like the sound of this at all, Fred,' he said. 'I am going to send you for a chest X-ray. Do you know where the clinic is in St George's Road?'

He explained where and when Fred had to attend and gave him a slip of paper to take with him. As Harriet showed him out of the front door, he said to her, quietly, 'You will see that he goes, won't you? It is very important we know what we're treating.'

'I will go with him, doctor,' she said. 'Thank you for calling in.'

The results of the X-ray were sent direct to Dr Purcell and he called again the following Saturday afternoon. By then Fred had admitted to himself that he wasn't feeling too good, the cough was getting him down. His skin had taken on an ashen hue and his face looked drawn.

When the doctor left, Fred and Harriet understood that he had lung cancer in both lungs. It was inoperable, there was nothing that could be done medically. Both of them felt that they had been felled by heavy blows.

Fred tried to continue as normal for a while, but had to give up work. His gardening was a source of solace to him for some time longer, but gradually that became too much and he had to retire to bed. At first Sheila would peep into his room and talk to him, but after a few weeks he scarcely seemed to notice she was there. She grew afraid of his silences and her visits ceased.

'I know you said Grandad has cancer but when will he get better?' eight-year-old Sheila asked her mother, after Fred had been bedridden for a number of weeks.

Edna took a deep breath; she had made it one of her principles never to lie directly to her children, there was no way round this direct question.

'I think we have to accept that Grandad is so ill he is not going to get better, but please don't say that to him, we don't want to upset him.'

Sheila nodded and said nothing. She tried not to cry or ask any more questions, deciding if she was to be treated as an adult she would act like an adult. So she didn't discuss it with her grandfather, as her mother had requested, and stopped praying to God each night to make him better, in fact, stopped praying at all.

Fred died two weeks later, he was sixty-three. With him went a gentleness, a quietness and a spirit of acceptance from the house. Harriet, Edna, Alice and Lilian consoled each other as best they could. The daughters marvelled at how strong their mother seemed.

'I've had several months to prepare myself for this,' she told them. 'Besides, he was so ill at the end I couldn't have wished him to continue. He was a good man and led a good life. He was a good husband to me and a wonderful father to all of you. I know he was very proud of you.' Fred had never made any distinction between his own daughter and Bill's daughters, and Harriet loved him for it.

As was still the custom, Fred was laid out in his coffin on trestles, in the front parlour, where he had taken so many Sunday afternoon naps in the past; the coffin was left open for relatives to call and pay their last respects. The day before the funeral, Harriet took Sheila into the front parlour.

'Come and say goodbye to your Grandad,' she said, 'the funeral is tomorrow.'

Sheila peeped into the coffin. It was her grandad, but his eyes were closed and he was very pale, even paler than when he had been ill. He was very still.

'Just put your hand on his forehead, feel how cold he is,' said Harriet, then noticing Sheila's reticence she added, 'He ain't going to hurt you. He never hurt you while he was alive, he certainly won't hurt you now he's dead.'

In the face of that irrefutable logic, Sheila laid her hand on her grandfather's forehead. Yes he was cold, how could people get that cold? He felt and looked like one of the marble statues on tombs in the church. And Grandma was right, there was nothing to be afraid of in death, dead people couldn't hurt you.

'Bye bye, Grandad,' she whispered and looked at Harriet who nodded to her.

On the day of the funeral it had been arranged that Joyce, who was now fifteen years old and soon to leave school, would have the day off school to look after Sheila and two-year-old Pat. Everyone else would attend the funeral. Harriet was in the front parlour, looking out of the window for the funeral cars when she suddenly called out to Edna, 'Would you believe it, here's old Isaac!' And sure enough, there was Fred's father striding up the road, his overcoat unbuttoned and flapping in the wind. He was ninety-two and had come by bus to attend his son's funeral. Harriet was astounded, but she and Edna welcomed him warmly and he was introduced to the grandchildren whom he had never seen before. Pat and Sheila were fascinated by him as he had a 'funny eye' as they both called it later; he had once been whitewashing a ceiling with lime when some splashed into his eye, burning it badly. It gave him the appearance of having a glass eye. The two children couldn't stop staring at him until Edna sent them to play in Sheila's bedroom.

After the funeral Harriet decided she should move out of the double bedroom so that Sheila and Pat could share that room; she would have the single room. The children were excited to think of sharing and Pat was thrilled to feel she was old enough to progress to a bed rather than a cot. Edna and Len had been looking for a house of their own until Fred's illness was diagnosed; to move out now and leave Harriet alone was out of the question.

Yewey continued to call on his rounds with his vegetables, although he confessed to Harriet it was all beginning to get too much for him now he was nearing seventy. This may have been one of the factors which influenced him to propose marriage to Harriet on one of his visits, although he was also genuinely fond of her.

'Oh, I don't think so, Yewey,' said Harriet hesitantly. 'Let me think about it.'

She told Edna about Yewey's proposal later that evening.

'Well mum, it's up to you,' said Edna, 'I think it will be more for his benefit than yours.'

That was also Harriet's analysis of the situation. The next time Yewey called at the house she told him, as kindly as she could, that she had decided not to marry again.

'I have had two husbands, I think three in one lifetime would be too many,' she concluded. At the end of the summer Yewey gave up his market garden and sold his pony and cart.

Harriet's life entered a period of quiescence. She delighted in her grandchildren and their achievements. She still found pleasure in visiting the seaside and she regularly rented a caravan at Brean during the summer holidays, always taking two or more of her grandchildren with her. She allowed them plenty of freedom during the day, as long as they were back for meals and did not swim in the sea unless she was present, as the mud and the tides were treacherous. The children grew to know the area well and enjoyed these holidays with their grandmother until they became too sophisticated for such simple pleasures.

Young Ken had finished school and found an office job in a large garage, which pleased him as he was more interested in cars than anything else in the world. Joyce too left school a few years after Ken and started work in Brights department store in Bristol. Little Pat was growing into a pretty, self-confident child and was soon to start school at the modern school which had been built nearby. Sheila had just passed her eleven-plus and was to start at the grammar school, much to Len's delight; he had spent many evenings coaching her in maths. Harriet was pleased to see that both Joyce and Sheila had inherited Harriet's ability to sew and make clothes from next-to-nothing—an aptitude which had bypassed all three of her daughters.

Edna and Len had taken over the day-to-day maintenance of the house and garden, so Harriet had none of those worries, but they had insisted on having both a telephone and central heating installed. Harriet welcomed the former, but had reservations about the heating, especially as so many holes had to be knocked in the walls to accommodate the pipes. However once it was all working she was won over; a warm bathroom—now that was a novelty!

Ellen's husband, Bill, died; Ellen came back to Bristol to live with her daughter and her husband. She and Harriet still visited each other from time to time.

Alice and Reg, meanwhile, had sold their house in Heath Road and taken a tenancy in a Bristol public house, the Wine Vaults in Park Row. It was a short bus ride from Harriet's house to the Wine Vaults so Harriet visited them most weeks. For the first few years the business was successful until the advent of television emptied the public houses for a few years, until the attraction of staying home watching television began to pale. By that time the brewery had closed the Wine Vaults and it became an antique shop.

'We can't buy another house, Ma, we lost so much money in the business,' said Alice to her mother. Harriet was upset; they had both worked so hard and it resulted in failure, through no fault of their own, just bad timing.

'Where will you go?' Harriet asked. 'And what will you do?'

'Reg is going for a job at the aircraft factory and his cousin has a cottage we can rent, at Oldbury-on-Severn. It's a bit of a journey from there to work for him, but he says he can manage. It's quite a big place, large rooms—we shall have to find some more furniture!'

'You can have my bedroom suite,' said Harriet immediately. 'It will do for your spare bedroom. I know Len is planning to build-in furniture in the children's bedroom. And there's that big mahogany chest on the landing, I'm sure Edna would prefer to have the space.'

Reg and Alice moved to the country, where Reg's family had

originated and where his sister now lived. Harriet went to visit them for a week's stay during the summer. Alice was right, it was a very attractive cottage in a pleasant village, but Harriet was surprised to find that there was no piped water to the house. There was a pump outside in the garden and a privy.

'We are having piped water laid on to the house soon, Ma, so it will be more modern then,' said Alice.

Harriet loved the peace of the countryside; it reminded her of when she and Bill Fricker had lived at Peasedown St John, then later at Hanham. Her brief sojorn at Bloomfield, with Ellen, had reawakened her love of rural life.

Ken stayed in Bristol, he had met and then married a young lady called Margaret. Margaret's family came from Pontypridd; her sister was fifteen years old, the same age as Sheila, so the two girls visited each other's homes. On Sheila's return from South Wales, Harriet asked her what she thought of her visit.

'It was good, I thoroughly enjoyed it. I've learned to sing the Welsh National Anthem in Welsh and I can make Welsh Cakes. But there were some funny things. We were going for a day out with some of Mair's friends, to the Folk Museum at St Fagans, I was wearing those new trousers mum bought me. The girls there don't ever wear trousers, but Mair persuaded me to wear them that day. As we went to get on the bus, the conductor stopped me and said 'I don't know if I can let you on, are you a boy or a girl?'

'How rude,' said Harriet. 'What did you say?'

'I stuck my chest out and said "If you don't know the difference, then I'm sorry for you" and we all got on the bus laughing. The boys especially.'

Harriet laughed, her grand-daughter so reminded her of herself at that age, but had more of the freedom Harriet would have liked. 'Nothing gets past you, does it?'

'Well, it is nineteen fifty-four, grandma, not the dark ages. Women wore trousers during the war years. Another thing, over there, women are not allowed in pubs; I don't know why women should be treated differently from men. And their pubs don't open at all on a Sunday.'

'No. I know that,' said Harriet. 'That's because they're nearly all Chapel. At one time chapel-goers didn't drink at all. Some of them still don't; others don't drink on a Sunday.'

Harriet too received an invitation to visit the family in South Wales for a week, taking Pat with her. Their week was pleasant but not as exciting as Sheila's stay. The charms of South Wales which Harriet had perceived on her visits to Crumlin seemed now to have deserted the mining areas.

The following year Lilian's daughter, Joyce, married her young man. Vic was a bus driver on the local bus route, so the family never had to walk home from a bus stop when Vic was driving; he dropped them at the end of Heath Road. Lilian was pleased that the young couple had managed to buy a house in the same road as herself; she had not been looking forward to losing her daughter. Edna, meanwhile, had been thinking of returning to work.

'Now the girls are growing up, they're both at school all day, there's no real need for me to be at home all the time,' she said to Len. 'The money would come in handy, we could buy a few little luxuries, like a television.' Edna and Harriet had for some time been discussing the desirability of a television set; Len was not strongly in favour, seeing it as timewasting.

'What job will you do, dear?' he asked, offering no objections to the main proposal.

'I would like to go back to nursing,' Edna replied decisively. 'I can't become a student nurse again, but I could work part-time as an auxiliary. Frenchay is our nearest hospital, and it's easy to get there.'

Edna applied, was accepted and started work. From the beginning she loved the hospital and her work there; Harriet was delighted to see her daughter so happy. They acquired a television set, which provided many hours of easy entertainment for Harriet, as she was becoming more sedentary. However she still saw herself as custodian of the family, much to the annoyance of Sheila and Pat. As they entered adolescence their boyfriends were carefully vetted. Both girls complained that if a boy walked them home after an evening out, they could see their grandmother's bedroom curtains twitching as she watched to see if there were any 'goodnight kisses'.

Ken and Margaret presented Harriet with her first great-grandchild, Susan, a pretty baby with dark hair and dark eyes, like Ken. Harriet sat in her easy chair, with the baby on her lap, thinking of all the babies she had held: her younger siblings, her own children, her grandchildren, and now a great-grandchild. She looked around her family, happily chattering in Edna's sitting room, and thought how fortunate she was now.

Sheila left school and found a job in advertising. Both Len and Edna had wanted their daughter to stay at school and apply for university, but that was not what she wanted at the time. In Harriet's eyes, Sheila had made the right decision, she still viewed the progression from a steady job to marriage as the desirable route for girls. After eighteen months in her first job she moved to a new agency, to work in public relations. It was here that she met Bob, and they were later married in Stapleton Church, the same church as her parents wedding had taken place over twenty-one years previously.

Harriet had given her grand-daughter a tea service as a wedding present, but called her into her bedroom one day and unwrapped a tissue paper parcel. It was a teapot, but not like any other teapot Sheila had ever seen. It had a wicker handle, and was made of earthenware, decorated with a blue oriental design.

'I would like you to have this; it was given to me by my grandmother when I was married, and I've always thought I would give it to you. It's not valuable, just sentimental value. Would you like it?'

'Yes of course I would,' Sheila kissed her grandmother. 'What a lovely idea, to pass it on from grandmother to grand-daughter. But I've never seen it before; where did you keep it?'

'Usually in one of the cupboards. I haven't put it out on show, it wouldn't go with your mother's things.'

'Too right,' said Sheila, putting the teapot with her store of wedding gifts and items she had made for her new home.

The following winter two more great-grandchildren arrived; Joyce's son, Robert, was born in November and Sheila's daughter, Kim, in December. Then at one year intervals, Ken's son, Andrew, was born followed by Sheila's second daughter, Tania, and finally Joyce's daughter, Alison.

'That's six great-grandchildren in as many years,' said Harriet, 'and all fit and well.' Memories of her mother, who had buried five babies of the ten she had borne, came flooding back to Harriet and she silently gave thanks for the improved healthcare and cleaner living conditions which enabled the decrease in infant mortality.

Harriet (on right) with Louise Rossiter (Edna's mother-in-law) on a daytrip to Weston-super-Mare; both ladies were in their seventies at this time.

Chapter 10

FINALLY

Harriet's life in her later years centered around her family, giving both practical and moral support. Her routines had never varied; she always wore an all-enveloping crossover pinafore at home. Every morning she rolled her hair into curlers, covering them with a scarf tied as a turban, and unrolled the curlers each afternoon, fashioning her hair into a roll secured by hairpins on the nape of her neck. She continued living with Edna and Len, while Alice and Lilian visited her at least once a week, although this entailed almost three hours travelling for Alice. Harriet enjoyed these visits which usually included several bouts of hilarious laughter; her daughters kept her up-to-date with their family news and Harriet offered her opinion, in her usual forthright manner, as to what course of action they should take. Alice was always extremely jovial and regaled them with jokes and entertaining accounts of people and incidents from the village where she and Reg lived. Joyce and Sheila were also regular visitors, bringing their children with them. Edna's other daughter, Pat, still lived at home; when she left school she had won a scholarship to The Bristol Old Vic Theatre School, to train as an actress.

Sheila was living in central Bristol, near the Downs; it was convenient to her husband's workplace and she was only a bus ride away from her mother and grandmother. Edna still worked three days a week, so Sheila usually visited on one of the days she was at home. Harriet was surprised therefore to receive a phone call from Sheila one morning when Edna was not at home, asking if her mother was there.

'No, she's at work today, my love, is there anything I can help with?' asked Harriet.

'I was just hoping she might have had the day off, Gran. I am feeling so ill, I've got a migraine and really need to lie down. It didn't start until after Bob had gone to work, and I can't get hold of him today.' Sheila's girls were three years and one-year old respectively.

Harriet thought for a moment. She had never suffered from migraine but Edna had, in the past, and Harriet knew how debilitating it was. Coping with two young children in those circumstances would be unbearable.

'I'll get the bus and come and look after the children for the day,' she said decisively. She had never been to the house by bus before; either Bob or Len had taken her by car when she visited. 'Tell me where to get off the bus and I'll be there in half an hour, buses willing.'

'Gran, are you sure?' Sheila was concerned; her grandmother was seventy-seven years old and not used to travelling by bus these days.

'Yes of course,' said Harriet. 'After all, there's no one else, everybody's at work.'

True to her word, Harriet arrived at Sheila's house within half an hour and looked after the girls all day, even managing to cook them some lunch on an electric cooker, when she had only ever used gas previously.

Sheila had inherited her grandmother's love of the countryside and in 1964 moved with her family to Frampton Cotterell, a rural area on the perimeter of Bristol. When Edna and Len were due to take their annual holiday Harriet opted to stay with Sheila's family for the week as she always enjoyed a week in the country. Sheila had recently started a degree course at the University of Bristol, having taken her entrance exams the previous summer, fulfilling her father's ambitions for her.

'I'm ten years older than the other students, must be a late starter,' she quipped.

Harriet was unsure of the value of a degree for a married woman with children, although she did not say so to Sheila.

'What will you do with a degree?' she asked.

'Probably go into teaching, Gran. I enjoyed running the playgroup, I like working with children. It's a good job, worthwhile, and I get the same holidays as my children. It also means that I don't have to take the usual rubbish jobs they offer to married women with children.'

Harriet concurred with the latter sentiment and saw the strength of Sheila's argument. Sheila and her girls prepared the spare room for Harriet and made her welcome, taking her breakfast in bed every morning.

'You don't have to bother to do all this for me, just a cup of tea would do,' she protested.

'No, Gran, think of this as your holiday. Besides, it's no trouble at all.' In fact it was easier for Sheila to make everyone's breakfast at the same time and take Harriet's, plus a pot of tea, on a tray to her room. Harriet enjoyed having all her meals cooked for her but she insisted on helping prepare the vegetables. 'The Devil finds work for idle hands' was still one of her favourite sayings. The weather was fine that week and Harriet spent a great deal of time sitting in the garden watching the children play.

Even into old-age Harriet remained a decisive and determined woman, but the scars of her early life had not made her callous to the suffering of others. She was devastated at the news of the 1966 Aberfan Disaster, when the mine's slag heap slipped and engulfed the local primary school and so many young children were killed. The following day Edna was looking after Kim and Tania, who were seven and five years respectively, and was teaching them to knit. She suddenly became aware that Harriet was watching from the doorway with tears rolling down her cheeks.

'Whatever is it, mum?'

'I was just thinking of all those children from Aberfan, their little hands stilled forever.' Harriet produced a hanky from the pocket of her wrapover pinafore, dabbed her eyes and went to the kitchen to make a pot of tea.

With advancing age Harriet rarely went farther than the local shops. As the winter of 1967 approached she began feeling 'under the weather', as she expressed it to Edna.

'Nothing specific, just not quite right. Suppose I must be getting old,' she said wryly, she was eighty-two at the time. 'I've never liked the winter much, don't know how we used to put up with it before we had central heating.'

There were no specific symptoms, but Harriet seemed unwell and later began to complain of a 'shaky stomach'. She had also begun to lose weight, but attributed this to the fact that she was not eating so well due to her feelings of nausea. She had seen their doctor but he could find nothing wrong.

'I've got no pain at all, just shaky, makes me feel a bit sick,' she told Edna. Edna was concerned that her mother was ill, and decided to leave work in order to look after her. She gave a month's notice at the hospital where she had worked for fifteen years and was now regarded as an indispensable member of staff.

The Assistant Matron was shocked. 'You are really going to give up your job, where you have done so well?' she asked Edna piercingly, almost accusingly. 'After all, you are more than fifteen years off retirement age.'

'Yes,' replied Edna. 'Whatever happens, I can always get another job but I can never get another mother.'

No further arguments could be posed to this and the senior nurse wished her well.

Harriet continued to decline; she still sat at the sink to prepare vegetables, which she considered as her task but had no energy for anything else. Edna went to see their doctor and asked him to send her mother to see a specialist. He diagnosed a growth in the stomach, which might or might not be malignant, and decided that Harriet should be admitted to Frenchay Hospital for tests; Edna found herself a visitor in the hospital where she had so recently worked.

Harriet was installed on a medical ward and her daughters and grandchildren visited her regularly; Edna and Sheila visited almost every day. The hospital was on Sheila's way home from University so she ensured she left early enough each afternoon to sit with her grandmother for half an hour before collecting her children from school; by this time she had managed to buy the Riley RME she had promised herself from childhood. Edna was often at the hospital when Sheila arrived. Two days a week Alice and Lilian would visit; Alice's bus only ran twice a week from Oldbury-on-Severn. The first week that Harriet was in hospital it was her eighty-third birthday and the ward provided her with a birthday cake; Harriet managed to eat a small slice with her afternoon cup of tea.

'Not as good as the cake you make,' she whispered to Edna who was sitting by her side, surrounded by other members of the family who had all sung 'Happy Birthday', joined by members of staff and patients.

Harriet did not take kindly to the tests and treatment she was receiving; she had only been in hospital once before in her life, for a skin complaint, and was not a willing patient. By the middle of her second week she asked Edna to arrange to take her home, the consultant was unwilling to operate on her, so what was the point of staying in hospital? She had picked up a cold, or chest infection, and was having difficulties breathing. Edna arranged to see Harriet's consultant to discuss her mother leaving hospital.

That afternoon when Sheila arrived at the hospital she found Edna, Alice and Lilian already present. Her grandmother was propped up on pillows, but seemed far worse than the previous day; her breath came in gasps, she could only manage one or two words at a time. Harriet's chest infection had turned to pneumonia.

After half an hour Sheila rose to leave; she was reluctant to go but had two children to collect from school.

'I must go now, Gran, because of the children.'

The old woman propped up on pillows nodded assent, her chest heaving, her breath coming in gasps, she was unable to speak in reply. Love merged with pity, Sheila put her arms around her grandmother and gave her a gentle hug, to the accompaniment of one of her aunts saying, 'Mind you don't catch anything, it's a germ she's got.'

That physical contact sealed their bond; in that moment Harriet knew and Sheila knew that they would never see each other again. Their eyes met as the young woman released her grasp and each realised that the other knew it was their last meeting.

'Goodbye, Gran.'

'Bye, love.'

Sheila would not permit herself tears in front of everyone but sat in her car two minutes later and cried as she had never cried before.

Harriet died next morning at half past seven. During her lifetime she had seen five British monarchs and two World Wars; transport had changed from horse-and-cart to jet aircraft. 'Ordinary people' were going abroad for holidays. From having a mother who could not read or write, she had a grandchild who was reading for a degree. The world had changed a great deal in Harriet's eighty-three years, especially the lives of women in Britain.

TRANSCRIPT OF FIRST WORLD WAR POSTCARDS

Fred Lewis sent postcards from:

10th Jy 1915: 12.50 p.m., Aldershot: Cartoon of soldier in uniform, inset of woman, verse.
Dear
Still another P.C hope you will like it went all over the place to get it
With Love Fred

23rd Jly (or possibly Jan, Jne?) **1915: 1p.m., Marlborough Lines, Aldershot:** picture of 'Airship sheds, Farnborough'
Dear wife
Just another PC for your album and I am sending the children one each hope they will like them
Yours for ever
Fred

23rd Au 1915: 10.45 a.m., Avonmouth: picture of 'Avonmouth new road entrance' (now called the Portway)
Dear
We are leaving for Southampton at 10.30 hope you got home alright I will send again soon
Fred xxxxx

18th Jan 1916: 11p.m., Folkestone: picture of Boulogne steamer leaving Folkestone harbour
*Dear
I have just arrived here and have to stay for the night there were too many for the boat,
Fred xxxxx*

17th Jul 1917: 2.30p.m., Folkestone: picture of 'The Leas Bandstand, Folkestone'
*Dear Wife
At this place going over today in the pink. With Love
Fred
xxxxx*

20th Sp 1918: Army Post Office: Italy: Picture of '(town name scratched out) Lido d'Aibaro – La Grotta al Mare'
*My Dear Wife
Just a P.Card hoping all are well and that I shall soon get a letter hope you got the other cards safe will send letter tomorrow
Best Love
Fred
xxx*

7th Oc 1918: Army Post Office: Italy: Picture of 'Galleria Mazzini' town name completely scratched out
*My Dear Wife
Just a P C as promise
Hope you and the children are quite well as it leaves me at present. Good Luck
With Love
Fred
xxx*

8th Oc 1918: Army Post Office: Italy: Picture of street with washing hanging across it on several levels. Town name scratched out 'Trugoli di

Santa Brigida'.
My Dear Wife
Just a P C letter to follow hope you are all quite well lovely weather here what about this for washing day good luck God Bless you and the children.
With Love
Fred
xxxxx

9th Oc 1918: Army Post Office: Italy: Picture of stately buildings and grounds. Town name scratched out, 'Camposanto'.
My Dear Wife
Just a P Card hope you will like it will answer your letter tomorrow grand weather what about the war our good luck
With love
Fred
xxx

12th Oc 1918: Army Post Office: Italy: Picture of seafront, town name bluepencilled but looks like Genoa, 'Via Circonvallazione a mare e Porto': Red stamp 'Passed by censor 474'
Dear Wife
Just a P.card to let you know I am alright still on the move will send letter as soon as possible hope all are in good health but love to all.
With Love
Fred
XXX

6th NOV ? 1918: Army Post Office: Italy: View of town: 'Saluti da (name scratched out) - Panorama'
My Dear Wife
(First two words now illegible) as promise hope all are quite well best love to you and the children

With Love
Fred xxx

The following were written and addressed but not stamped (enclosed with a letter, or taken home later?

Town name blue pencilled: Brossiecco, Padua ? (Via Mandriola Bassuhello) street scene, building with clock.
Well Dear
As you see by this P C there are fine buildings in this country sorry it's not a birthday card
With Love
Fred x
Xxxxx
(On address panel)*Dear*
There is one thing I forgot in my letter would you mind sending me a couple of views of Bristol I will let you know what I want them for in my next letter

Genova, Stazione Brignole
Dear Wife
(Field stamp obliterated most of brief message)
well and
with love
Fred
xxx

Oneglia, Panorama da ponento? (Blue pencilled but almost legible)
Dear
A P.C I had gave me I don't know wher it is but somewhere in this country
Love
Fred xxx

'Union is strength' (cartoon of flags) Field postal stamp

HARRIET'S FAMILY

Dear Wife
1(?) more P. Card hope you and the children are quite well. With Love
Fred xxx
Embroidered birthday card: Happy Birthday
Many Happy Returns of the Day. Good Luck
May you see a good many more
With Love
Fred xxxx

And brought home cards from:

Paris
Venice
Rome
Boulogne-sur-Mer
Genova
Bailleul
London
Eddystone lighthouse
Arras (before and after bombardment)
Vicentino
Albert (Somme) before and after bombardment
Southsea
Lake Como
Portsmouth
Book of cards of Arras after the bombs

Remembrance card from Harriet to Fred: 'Thoughts of you'
Picture and a verse.
Dear Fred
Just a card in remberance hope you are quite well hope you will like it
Yours ever
(no signature)

SHEILA HAYWARD

Extra cards found later

Buona Pasqua (Doves and Egg)
My dear wife
Just a P.C. I hope you will like it, it means good Easter hope I shall spend the next with you. Just had a letter from George quite well but fed up. Cheer up God Bless. You kiss the children for me hope to be with you soon. With Great Love Fred xxxxx (no address/date stamp)

Francais souvenons-nous! La France reconquise (1917) – PERONNE (name almost obliterated by pencil) Maisons Saccagees par les brutes prussiennes Havoc home's by the German Brutal's (their translation on the card!)
Dear
Put these with the rest will send two more next week. Fred xxxxxx (no address/date stamp)
(Also a second card of ruins of Peronne, no writing or address)

'Ebe??e Felice' Celebration card (couple and daughter holding a bottle and glass)
Postmarked Nov 6 1918 BFPO G?2
Mrs F. Lewis 22 Bloy Street Easton Bristol England
Dear Wife
Just a Post Card hope you will like it don't forget the bottle how about this for when I come home all over out here hope colds are better
With Love
Fred xx

'Absent yet near' Picture of woman writing to a soldier, small inset picture
Dear Fred
I send just a PC hope you will like it. best Love from your ever loving Wife
Hope you will be home soon dear Write soon dear xxxxxx (no address)

184

A souvenir from Aldershot (five small scenes)
From Fred your Loving Husband
Good luck God Bless you and the children xxxxxx (no address)

Remembrance of France (looks like hand-painted card, violets and scene, possibly sent as Birthday?)
Dear
I hope you will like this best I could get
Fred xxxxx

VERDUN Soldiers clearing the Streets after German Bombardment (on back: Official photograph of Section Photographique de l'Armee Francaise issued by NewspaperIllustrated Ltd 161a Strand, W.C. VERDUN – Soldiers clearing the streets after German bombardment. High explosive shells are now incessantly being fired into the town and men of the Territorials constantly keep the lines of communication free of the broken masonry and refuse.)
Dear Wife
In London for the night will explain later just having a good feed with Love Fred xxx
London postmark 12.15am 17 July 1916

Picture PC of man and woman and flowers
Dear
Hope you will like this it makes me think of the time before the war hoping we shall soon be together again. With Greatest Love Fred xxx

'Dear my heart' (Woman looking in mirror, verse about being apart)
Dear Fred
Just this card in return I hope you will like it from Your Loving Wife

Photo card of soldier standing by ambulance
Printed by K. Nicol & Co., 5 Waldemar Road, Wimbledon Park, S.W. (no writing/address/stamp)

SHEILA HAYWARD

'Bonne Annee' (picture of little girl with bunch of flowers)
Watten le 30+ 1917
Cher Alfred
Merci pour votre bonne carte elle nous a fait grand plaisir, je ?oins ainsi que ma famille mas souhait do bonne annee voeux de bonheur pour vous et les votres la paix dans la courant de cette annee – 1918. Bien souvent nous causons(?) de vous, pour laissioment (?) ici c'est tres clame (?) il y a au moins 20 centimetres de neige il fait tres froid et en Italie comment vous trouvez cette en droite l'hiver aussi, je close cette carte en vous souhaitant une bonne fin d'annee et bon commencement maman adrienne Blanche
Roughly translated and punctuation added:
Dear Alfred (!)
Thank you for your nice card it gave us great pleasure; I (send), also my family, many wishes for a good new year, wishes of happiness for you and yours, peace in the coming year – 1918. We very often (think) of you, for (?) . Here it is very calm, there is less than 20 cms of snow, it is very cold. And in Italy, how do you find it in the middle of winter also. I close this card and wish you a good end to the year and good beginning. Mother Adrienne Blanche (not sure if these are 2 or 3 people, only know of two, mother and daughter)

Double postcard: (1) ALBERT – Somme – Basilique de n.-D. de Brebieres (2) same view after bombardment) Guerrre 1914-1916
Dear
This is what I have seen lately on our travels but we do not go very often there
Fred xxxxxx   (no address/date)

BIBLIOGRAPHY

Arthur, M. *Forgotten Voices of the Great War,* Edbury Press, London, 2002

Black, Jeremy, *The Making of Modern Britain,* Sutton Press, Stroud, 2001

Buchanan, A & Cossons, N. *Industrial Archeology of the Bristol Region,* David & Charles, Newton Abbott, 1969

Bristol Times and Record, May 25th 1911, for the account of the Hanham Mine disaster inquest

Dike, John, *Bristol Blitz Diary,* Redcliffe Press, Bristol, 1982

Eveleigh, David J., *Bristol 1850 – 1919,* Sutton Press, Stroud, 1997

Eveleigh, David J., *Bristol 1920 –1969*, Sutton Press, Stroud, 1998

Forty, S. (Ed.) *World War I,* PRC Publishing, London, 2002

Harrison, David, (Ed.) *Bristol Between the Wars,* Redcliffe Press, Bristol, 1984

Hill, Maureen, *Britain at War: Unseen Archives,* Parragon, Bath, 2001

Liddell Hart, B.H., *History of the First World War (*3rd *ed.),* Pan Books,

London, 1972

Thomas, Ethel, *War Story,* E. Thomas, 1989

Thomson, David, *England in the Twentieth Century (1914-1963),* Penguin, Harmondsworth, 1969

The Bristol Picture Book (Part 2), Bristol Broadsides, Bristol (1987)

Winstone, Reece, (Ed), *Bristol's History, Vol 2,* R.J. Ackford, Chichester, 1975

Winstone, Reece, *Bristol in the 1880s,* Burleigh Press, Bristol, 1962

HOW I RESEARCHED THIS BOOK

When my Grandmother died I determined to write her life story: she had experienced an interesting, if turbulent, life very different from my own. When I was a child she had regaled me with stories of her childhood; I had lived with her for the first twenty years of my life, so I knew her very well. I began writing shortly after her death, then realised how few facts I knew about her early life. At that time, with a full-time job and family I had no time to research the events properly.

On taking retirement six years ago I began my research and my book in earnest. It had to be put on hold for a year whilst we moved house, but then I picked it up again.

The real prompt to my research was finding the photograph of the Bolt family included in Chapter 1, followed by hearing a talk by Pat Hase on researching family history.

Information from family members

Never underestimate the importance of information held by other members of the family. I was fortunate in having three members of my family in their eighties, all with excellent memories and a fund of stories, and a cousin who has never thrown away a family photograph. She also knew the names of all the people in the photos! On showing my Bolt family photo to relatives many other family photos were given me. I was beginning to build a visual picture.

The research

I began by visiting the so-called local history section of Bristol Library, in 2002. The staff were less than helpful, the facilities primitive by today's standards. Everything was on microfilm or microfiche and there were no indexes available. I spent hours screening births on microfiche—don't bother! I knew my grandmother was born in 1885 so would have been named on the 1901 census and that her family lived in Bedminster. I spent a whole afternoon finding them on the microfilm; nowadays you can look at the *1901 census online*, much quicker and easier. If you do not have internet facilities, your *local library* will let you use theirs, as will your *local family history society*. They will be more than helpful and are full of enthusiasts who usually know the best way to find what you are looking for. I found the *Weston-super-Mare Family History Society* before I found the Bristol one; they were very helpful and provided a much-needed boost to my morale.

Having found where my family was living in 1901 I looked in the old Bristol *Street Directories* to confirm that they were living 'over the shop'. I followed the street directories backwards and forwards in time to confirm when they moved into the shop and when they moved out.

I now knew the names of my great-grandparents and decided to buy copies of their birth certificates. I went to the *Bristol Registry Office* to ask for them, having a rough idea of when they were born from the ages given on the 1901 census. The clerk at the Registry told me there were two George Bolts, one registered four years before the other. It was likely, she said, that the first baby had died and the second was given the same name, which was a typical Victorian practice. It was then that I realised there would be hidden names to research, those who died at birth or in infancy. I paid my fee and booked a half-day's research at the Registry Office, which would give me access to the birth and death indexes. That was how I discovered my great-grandmother had lost five other full-term children as well as the five who were in the photograph. I returned to the Registry a number of times throughout my research in order to investigate branches of the family.

The two birth certificates I ordered gave me the names and occupations of the parents of my great-grandparents. Armed with this information I was able to look for them on previous censuses; even in my early days the *1881 census* was online, on the Mormon site, and I found it invaluable. It was here that I found my great-grandmother had ostensibly married again. I checked a film copy of the *1871 census* (at least there was an index to help me by then) and found that her husband was not entered on the census, although she was still listed as married, not widowed, but Head of Household. I simply assumed this was an Enumerator's mistake, as old censuses are full of them. Imagine my surprise when, on checking the 1901 census again I found her living with her first husband again, in Gloucester. I have still not solved the mystery of where he went for twenty years; I checked prison records, even Australian deportation records and voluntary emigrations, but no trace. He had not appeared on any census forms under his own name. Possibly he went abroad or simply lived in this country under an assumed name. I will find out one day. I also checked the 'deaths' online on a site called *FreeBMD*, to find that the man she had been living with had died before she returned to her first husband. FreeBMD is a slightly temperamental site which was vastly overused and froze regularly but I was on a tight budget and found it very useful. I checked a number of my family's births, marriages and deaths on this site. When I needed more details I purchased certificates from the Registry. As most of my family were born, lived and died in Bristol I could obtain these in person. This is cheaper and quicker than ordering online or by post from the *General Registry Office* in London; they have now moved in with the National Archives, so all is under one roof.

I bought a copy of the Bristol *1851 Census* on disk, which has been invaluable in tracing many branches of the family. Nowadays all the censuses are available online, my advice is don't try to do too much in one sitting.

Another source for checking births, marriages and deaths, as well as indexed copies of census returns from 1841 to 1901 was the *Bristol Records Office*. All counties and most cities have their own Records Offices. I found Bristol especially competent and helpful; in addition there is the advantage that the *Bristol and Avon Family History Society* have a research room there which is staffed by knowledgeable volunteers at specific times.

My Grandmother had told me that her first husband had been killed in a mining accident at Hanham. I contacted the *Hanham Family History Society*, who took my cousin and me on a tour of the remnants of the old mine, and later put me in touch with a descendant of the other man killed in the same accident. From this source I obtained a copy of the newspaper account of the accident and inquest, which I had been unable to find. It's good to share, and I was very grateful.

When I came to research the First World War I went to *The National Archives at Kew*. The staff there are very knowledgeable and helpful. I consulted the medals rolls, campaign maps and—most enlightening—accounts of the war by company commanders, which gave insight on the day-to-day lives of the soldiers. Unfortunately most of the 'other ranks' individual records were burnt in a WW2 blitz, apart from the Medal Rolls.

I am an avid reader and read every book I could find on old Bristol; some of the WW2 books provided me with facts I would not have known. Those which provided me with information I have used I have listed in the Bibliography. All helped me to feel the ambiance of the era.

When I had completed my factual research I then interwove the family stories I knew and others told me by family members. Some I had to discount as fiction, as there were no facts to substantiate them. I keep those in my mind still, in case I find they applied to other generations or other as yet unknown family members. I may have finished the book but I have not given up research!

Useful websites

www.familysearch.org This is the Mormon site

www.1901census.nationalarchives.gov.uk

www.freeBMD.org.uk

www.nationalarchives.gov.uk/documentsonline/medals

www.gro.gov.uk This is the General Registry Office site

www.churchcrawler.co.uk if churches feature in your research, as they did in mine.

ISBN 1425177840